Casualty Aversion and Force Protection

The Shaping of American Strategy and Military Doctrine

James Roth, editor

ISBN -13: 978-1475133486
ISBN-10: 1475133480

Introduction

At the turn of the last century, military analysts began to notice U.S. strategy selection seemed driven by casualty risk, with optimal strategies being those that yielded the fewest potential killed, wounded, and missing.

In other words, the military yield of a strategy was subordinated to casualty considerations and these considerations appeared exaggerated, if not outlandish at the time.

it is tempting to view this debate as over and settled but even the most casual observer sees the obsession with "force protection" living on. "Force protection" had soldiers "patrolling" Baghdad in armored vehicles racing at 50 miles an hour through civilian neighborhoods. It had infantry soldiers encased in sandbag prisons wearing heavy protective armor in 120 degree heat trying to be effective at something no one could reasonably define.

The author of the Iraq surge and Afghanistan counterinsurgency, Gen. David Petraeus, evicted soldiers from their high-speed taxis and their bunkers but in doing so, he encountered the deep cultural resistance of the military and political orders.

Today, the excesses of the force protection mentality have found an additional outlet - civilian casualty minimization. When Petraeus put soldiers in contact with civil society, the extraordinary restrictions on use of deadly force were allowed to stand. Soldiers, less "force protected" themselves, were in a kind of "lockdown mode" with respect to how and when they could use their weapons against attacks. The grotesque aspects of this were lost on the military and civilian hierarchies, who

3

were responding supremely powerful cultural and political requirements.

Every reasonable person may agree that Petraeus has retired and his policies will eventually retire with him. This spells a return to the more extreme force protection policies in tandem with continued civilian protection measures that heavily restrict whom may shoot at what and under which circumstances.

While the essays that follow focus on the pathology of the force protection ethos, for those who make and uphold these policies there are tremendous potential benefits.

A force that does no harm and does not suffer harm itself can be deployed at supremely low levels of political cost. Assuming it can accomplish any policy ends on that basis, it gives politicians and generals one more option in geopolitics. This seems to those in power a compelling reason to distort (damage?) the military culture, ethos, and capability.

Jeffrey Record initiated this discussion with FAILED STATES AND CASUALTY PHOBIA. What follows are more or less reactions to and elaboration of the views expressed in this paper.

The material here is organized in chronological sequence, which allows readers to follow the arguments more easily.

The thread of these arguments are too important to consign them to the history bin. Force protection and its impetus remain with us today.

Contents

Introduction 3

FAILED STATES AND CASUALTY PHOBIA 7

Implications for Force Structure and Technology Choices 7

    I. INTRODUCTION 8

    II. FAILED STATES...9

    III. CASUALTY PHOBIA 17

    IV. IMPLICATIONS FOR FORCE STRUCTURE AND
    TECHNOLOGY CHOICES 25

Force-Protection Fetishism 51

Sources, Consequences, and (?) Solutions....................51

    Clausewitz Corrupted..53

    The Corrupting Agent: The Weinberger-Powell Doctrine......55

    Public Opinion and Casualties..............................57

    Strategic Consequences of the Elite's Casualty Phobia 61

    Remedies for Force-Protection Fetishism?............................66

Politics, Death, and Morality in US Foreign Policy 69

    Behind the Cult 71

    Making a Virtue of Timidity................................73

    Reassessing the Morality of War 75

    Making Moral Strategy 77

Casualty Aversion...79

    Implications for Policy Makers and Senior Military Officers..79

    Casualties and Public Opinion..............................82

    The Casualty Myth 91

Implications for Policy Makers 94

Implications for Senior Military Leaders 97

Conclusion 102

The Casualty-Aversion Myth 105

AMERICAN CASUALTY SENSITIVITY 106

Myth and Conventional Wisdom 107

THE NUANCED REALITY 112

NEGATIVE EFFECTS OF CASUALTY-AVERSION ASSERTION ... 115

Inefficient or Ineffective Execution 116

MASS VERSUS ELITE OPINION 118

Emboldening Adversaries 123

Casualty/Technology Trade-offs 126

Self-Constraint in the Use of Armed Forces 128

POLICY APPLICATIONS 130

Latitude for Leadership 130

The Cost-Benefit Policy Equation 133

The Professional Military Ethic 135

CONCLUSION 137

FAILED STATES AND CASUALTY PHOBIA

Implications for Force Structure and Technology Choices

by Jeffrey Record

Occasional Paper No. 18, Center for Strategy and Technology, Air War College Air University, Maxwell Air Force Base, Alabama

This influential paper was first published in September 2000. Record taught at the Air War College and Record and this work tended to reinforce his reputation as a defense policy critic. He served as a civilian advisor in the Mekong Delta during the Vietnam War, and subsequently as research associate at the Brookings Institution, then legislative assistant to Senator Sam Nunn, and senior fellow at the Institute for Foreign Policy Analysis, Hudson Institute, and the BDM International Corporation. Published under the auspices of the USAF, these do not represent the views of the U.S. Government.

I. INTRODUCTION[1]

The emergence of failed states as the principal source of international political instability and the appearance of mounting casualty phobia among U.S. political and military elites have significant force structure and technology implications. Overseas, intra-state and often irregular warfare is displacing large-scale inter-state conventional combat. At home, there has arisen a new generation of political and military leadership that displays an unprecedented timidity in using force.

Yet the Pentagon continues to prepare to refight the Korean and Gulf Wars—simultaneously, no less!—and to invest heavily in force structures whose commitment to combat would invite politically unacceptable casualties. The air war over Serbia should be a warning to U.S. force planners: In contingencies not involving direct threats to manifestly vital U.S. interests—the post-Cold War norm, elevation of force protection to equal or greater importance than mission accomplishment mandates primary, even exclusive reliance on air power. It further

---

[1]. This monograph draws on several of the author's recent works, including: "Foreign Policy Incoherence and Military Timidity: Sources and Consequences," *Strategic Review* (Fall 2000); "From Tet to Kosovo: How Defeat in Vietnam Altered America's Use of Force Overseas," *The Long Term View* (Summer 2000); "Force Protection Fetishism: Sources, Consequences, and (?) Solutions," *Aerospace Power Journal* (Summer 2000); "Operation Allied Force: Yet Another Wake-Up Call for the Army?", *Parameters* (Winter 1999-2000); *Serbia and Vietnam, A Preliminary Comparison of the U.S. Decisions to Use Force* (Center for Strategy and Technology, Air War College, 1998); and *The Creeping Irrelevance of U.S. Force Planning* (Strategic Studies Institute, U.S. Army War College, 1998).

mandates expanded investment in stand-off precision-strike munitions and other technologies providing greater range and accuracy. The Army's combat arms were more or less irrelevant to the war against Serbia because of that service's comparative strategic immobility, and because a casualty-phobic White House and Pentagon leadership had already decided to withhold U.S. ground combat forces from exposure to combat. Yet the war—against a tiny, isolated, third-rate military power—consumed almost one-half the Air Force's deployable combat assets. The defense budget debate of recent years has predictably focused on the scope and wisdom of the post-Cold War cuts in overall defense spending. But the debate has unfortunately sidestepped what is perhaps an even more important issue—namely, the continued sharing out of defense dollars in roughly equal amounts to the various services against the backdrop of dramatically altered international and domestic political landscapes. "Enough of What?" is just as important a defense budget question as "How Much is Enough?"

II. FAILED STATES

At the beginning of the twentieth century, the international political system was dominated by a half-dozen European great powers and Japan. Most of what subsequently became known as the Third World was governed from colonial offices in London, Paris, Lisbon, and Amsterdam. The primary source of instability in a system so constituted was great power rivalry in Europe and overseas. Indeed, with the formation of the modern state in the wake of the Treaty of Westphalia (1648), great power war became the scourge of the international political system, and it was waged with increasing ferocity in the wake of the French and Industrial Revolutions.

Since 1945, the international political system has dramatically changed. War seems to have disappeared altogether among advanced industrial states; Europe, the cockpit of large-scale interstate warfare for three centuries, has become a continent of near-universal peace. Explanations for this unexpected phenomenon abound, but most observers believe that Europe's "pacification" is a function of some combination of economic integration, democratization, and war's utter discreditation as a means of settling disputes among states. Michael Mandelbaum believes that sovereign states "remain a central presence in human affairs at the end of the twentieth century. But in the societies that waged the modern era's major wars, the state has found a different purpose....The test of the legitimacy of governments [in these states] is likely to be economic rather than military. The Soviet Union was not defeated on the field of battle. It collapsed from within, in no small part because of economic failures."[2] John Mueller argues convincingly that the "psychic costs of war have increased dramatically over the last 200 years or so...in the developed world. Where people once saw great glory and honor in war—and particularly in victory— they are now often inclined to see degradation in it instead as war has increasingly come to be regarded as an enterprise that is immoral, repulsive, and uncivilized."[3]

---

[2] .Michael Mandelbaum, "Is Major War Obsolete?", *Survival* (Winter 1998-1999), p. 25.

[3] . John Mueller, *Quiet Cataclysm, Reflections on the Recent Transformation of World Politics* (New York: Harper Collins, 1995, p. 34. Also see Michael Mandelbaum, *The Dawn of Peace in Europe* (New York: Twentieth Century Fund Press, 1996).

Russia and Switzerland excepted, all of Europe's significant industrial states are members of the European Union, NATO, or both, and a war within either organization is inconceivable. This certainly does not rule out the possibility of war by EU and NATO members against outside states; members of both participated in the Persian Gulf War, and eight years later NATO fought its only war ever against Serbia. The point is not that Europe has become free of violence, but rather that it has become free of major inter-state war. All of the continent's significant military powers, Russia again excepted, are now in economic and political-military alliance with each other and are likely to remain so for the foreseeable future.

If Europe's pacification removes what, for the three centuries preceding the end of World War II, was the world's primary source of large-scale inter-state warfare, the emergence of weak and failed states has dramatically elevated the relative incidence of lesser, intra-state warfare. Such states are the products of three waves of imperial disintegration that have flooded the international system with over two-hundred new states, many of them frail or altogether unviable. The first wave was World War I's destruction of the Hapsburg and Ottoman empires. The second was World War II's destruction of Europe's vast overseas colonial empires. The third was the Cold War's destruction of the Soviet empire in Eastern Europe and then of the Soviet Union itself.

All three waves produced states of questionable political and economic sustainability. The disappearance of imperial authority was often replaced by weak national political authority and in some cases even anarchy. Once-popular post-colonial regimes proved economically incompetent and sank into a mire of venality. And the arbitrary colonial boundaries that the new states inherited provided a source of disorder because they cut across tribal and ethnic lines as well as language and economic patterns.

Nor does disintegration appear to have halted. Successor states to empires continue to disintegrate in Africa, Southeastern Europe, the Caucasus, South Asia, and Southeast Asia.[4] It is an even bet that Indonesia and the Republic of South Africa will go the same way as the former Yugoslavia. Equally questionable is the long-term viability of the many Arab states whose governments have failed repeatedly to deliver to their mushrooming masses more than the barest minimum of economic and social security, to say nothing of political freedom.

Iraq is a major case in point. The country is a failed state by virtue of the strategic incompetence of its leadership in starting two disastrous wars and because of a decade of effective international economic sanctioning. Its infrastructure is all but gone, its wealth destroyed or looted, its air space patrolled by hostile aircraft, and its Kurdish North transformed into a foreign military protectorate. Indeed, the Gulf War never really ended; it is simply being continued at a much lower level of violence.

---

[4]. For a discussion failed states and their implications for the nature of war in the post-Cold War era, see Martin van Creveld *The Transformation of War* (New York: Free Press, 1991); Michael Ignatieff, *Blood and Belonging, Journeys Into the New Nationalism* (New York: Farrar, Straus and Giroux, 1993); Philippe Delmas, *The Rosy Future of War* (New York: Free Press, 1995; Robert D. Kaplan, *The Ends of the Earth, A Journey to the Frontiers of Anarchy* (New York: Random House, 1996); and Mary Kaldor, *New Wars and Old Wars, Organized Violence in a Global Era* (Cambridge, UK: Polity Press, 1999).

Consider also the inevitable emergence of a Palestinian state, which seems destined to be a failure absent—perhaps even in spite of—massive injections of international capital. Political divisions within the Palestinian community are severe, as they are within Israel, the chief enemy of a Palestinian state. Successful statehood presupposes not only success in dealing with enormous economic and social challenges but also Palestinian and Israeli leadership willing and able to curb die-hard extremists on both sides. These are tall orders.

To repeat, strong states are no longer the problem; weak ones are. Failed states have become the primary source of instability in the international political system, not just because war within the advanced industrial world has drastically receded, but also because failed states invite intervention by stronger states. State failure inherently attracts humanitarian intervention even when no strategic interest is present. But because the United States and its allies also have a strong stake in the present global political and economic order, they therefore have a strong stake in containing state failures' potentially adverse regional and strategic consequences. Thus the United States invaded Haiti not just to restore democracy but also to stanch the flow of unwanted Haitian refugees into America. Thus NATO moved against Serbia in 1999 not just to stop the ethnic cleansing of Kosovo but also to preserve the Alliance's own credibility and to prevent Southeastern Europe's further destabilization.

As the world's sole remaining superpower, the United States military today performs on a global basis essentially the same imperial policing task that the British military performed within the British empire. To be sure, the rest of the world is hardly a formal, territorial empire of the United States. But there is an

American empire nonetheless: informal, voluntarily associated, and resting on political and cultural attraction as much as on military and financial clout. Scores of states and hundreds of millions of people around the world look to the United States for leadership and security, and it is in America's strategic interest that they do so.

Predictions are always dangerous in international politics, but the Gulf War of 1991 *may* be the last of its kind for the United States. Saddam Hussein did not expect war with America when he invaded Kuwait. But his crushing defeat established U.S. conventional military supremacy for all the world to see, and it is difficult to imagine a non-Western state being so obtuse as to challenge the United States on its own military terms. Asymmetric approaches to neutralizing or defeating American military power are the most appealing way of doing so—a point acknowledged in the Pentagon's *Joint Vision 2020*.[5] Such approaches worked in South Vietnam, Lebanon, and Somalia—all failed states—and came close to working in NATO's war against Serbia—a failing if not yet failed state. During the past decade, the Pentagon has been called upon to intervene in or against one failing or failed state after another—Somalia, Haiti,

---

[5]. "We have superior conventional warfighting capabilities and effective nuclear deterrence today, but this favorable military balance is not static. In the face of such strong capabilities, the appeal of asymmetric approaches and the focus on the development of niche capabilities will increase. By developing and using approaches that avoid U.S. strengths and exploit potential vulnerabilities using significantly different methods of operation, adversaries will attempt to create conditions that effectively delay, deter, or counter the application of U.S. military capabilities." *Joint Vision 2020* (Washington, D.C.: U.S. Government Printing Office, June 2000), p. 6.

Bosnia, Serbia, and where it has encountered resistance, it has been resistance offered by non-state actors operating unconventionally or state actors pursuing non-military strategies to reduce potential U.S military effectiveness.

None of this is to argue that the United States can dispense with preparation for large-scale conventional war with other states. The history of international politics is full of surprises. Maintaining conventional military supremacy deters in the short-term and offers long-term insurance against the emergence of aspiring military peer competitors. To abandon preparation for conventional warfare would simply invite others to return to it. Moreover, the possibility of conventional war on the Korean Peninsula, in the Persian Gulf, and across the Taiwan Strait cannot be entirely dismissed. In each of these areas, however, adversaries are conclusively outclassed by the United States and its allies. Regional conventional military balances have turned decisively against North Korea, Iraq, and Iran. Moreover, China's potential to become a military competitor of the United States anytime soon has been significantly oversold by Cold War defense policy refugees and defense industry hucksters.[6] America's lead over both enemies and allies alike in the so-called "revolution in military affairs" is widening and may become unassailable because potential competitors are unable or unwilling to make the necessary investment in capital and talent.

Even were China eventually to emerge in the coming decades as a hostile, military peer competitor—a postulation that itself

---

[6]. See Chalmers Johnson, "In Search of a New Cold War," *Bulletin of Atomic Scientists* (September/October 1999), pp. 44-51.

rests on a questionable host of assumptions,[7] a Sino-American war likely would be predominately, even exclusively, a naval and air contest. These are arenas in which the comparative U.S. conventional military advantage over China is likely to remain the strongest. Avoidance of ground war on the Asian mainland has long been a wise strategic injunction for the United States, whose strategic position in East Asia since 1945 has always rested on offshore and peninsular friends and allies. Moreover, for the foreseeable future it is difficult to imagine a Sino-American causus belli other than a forcible Chinese attempt to place Taiwan under mainland control. Taiwan's defense, of course, is first and foremost a sea and air challenge, only secondarily a ground one.

What the Pentagon calls "stability operations" in weak or failed states is likely to consume significant U.S. military resources as long as such states remain the primary source of instability and war in the world. Technology may change *how* America fights in

---

[7]. The postulation presumes *all* of the following: the presence of historically unfounded Chinese imperial ambitions beyond East Asia; renewed Chinese double-digit annual GDP growth rates that vanished in 1997; continued autocracy in Beijing notwithstanding the information revolution, the emergence of a large middle class, and the growing material corruption of the communist elite; and the ability of any national government in China to accommodate explosive economic and social change. China-as-the-new-Soviet-Union also ignores China's critical dependence on the global capitalist economy. Unlike the Soviet Union, post-Mao China has sought not economic autarky but rather integration in the international economic order. It is far more dependent on foreign markets than the Soviet Union ever was and has amassed huge trade surpluses with the United States. China's stake in world trade would be threatened by any military confrontation with the United States and its East Asian allies.

the future, but it is change in the international political system that will determine *who* and *why* America fights. The United States achieved global military prominence in three victorious world wars (two hot, one cold) against other great powers, but all three of those wars had an unintended byproduct: the recurring subdivision of relatively stable empires into ever larger numbers of ever smaller national entities often beset from within by the threat of anarchy. There were 51 signatories to the United Nations Treaty in 1945, a number that has more than quadrupled since then.

III. CASUALTY PHOBIA

If small wars within failing or failed states have dominated demands on U.S. military power since the Cold War's demise, a mounting aversion to incurring American casualties—and to inflicting enemy civilian and even military casualties—has come to dominate use-of-force decision-making in the United States. This aversion has been especially pronounced with respect to intervention in small wars, because such wars rarely involve direct threats to manifestly vital U.S. interests. Intervention is usually conducted in the general interest of global order and stability and often involves politically messy military enforcement of "peace" on those who have no vested interest in it. As such, public tolerance for such interventions and their potential for casualties is dramatically lower—or at least believed to be so by political and military elites—than for war on behalf of "real" interests. Even those committed to the use of force on behalf of promoting American values as opposed to protecting U.S. strategic interests take the pessimistic view that the American people are unwilling to accept significant casualties on behalf of toppling dictators, terminating genocide, and restoring civil order. This pessimism in turn has bred an

American military timidity traditionally uncharacteristic of great power behavior and ultimately injurious to protection of U.S. strategic interests.

Elite casualty phobia, manifest for at least a decade but never more glaringly than in the war against Serbia, has been much discussed in recent years. The fact of elite casualty phobia is not in dispute; it is reflected in the Pentagon's obsession with force protection and confirmed by recent polling data. There is, moreover, substantial evidence that both political and military elites have convinced themselves that the American public's intolerance is significantly higher and more intractable than is actually the case. Elites nonetheless make the use-of-force decisions.

A strong aversion to casualties is, of course, rooted in American history and political culture. Americans value the individual much more than they do the state, and they have always sought, and with considerable success it might be added, to substitute technology for blood in battle. But only recently has aversion become, at least in the minds of those making war and peace decisions, a phobia—i.e., an aversion so strong as to elevate the safety of American troops above the missions they are assigned to accomplish. Casualty aversion is healthy; casualty phobia is not. Ironically, the phobia has been strengthened by the Persian Gulf War and even more so by the war against Serbia, both of which have suggested the possibility of war with little or no American death.

The phobia is rooted in the Vietnam War, which has produced a generation of political and military leaders that is much more reluctant to use force, or at least use it effectively, than those for whom Munich and World War II were the great foreign policy exemplars. The message of Munich was the imperative of using force early and decisively against aspiring conquerors; the perceived message of Vietnam is that the risks—both battlefield and domestic political—of using force almost always outweigh the benefits. Much of the present U.S. political elite is suspicious of the very legitimacy of force, and therefore considerably ill at ease in using it.[8]

Ironically, this uneasiness borders on distress among much of the U.S. military leadership, especially that of the Army, which is still in the grips of the Vietnam Syndrome. The Pentagon's determination to avoid repetition of that war even on the smallest of scales prompted implementation in the 1970s of the Total Force Policy, which was designed primarily to compel presidents to clear the domestic political hurdle of a reserve call-up before marching the country into a major war. The Total Force Policy was followed in the 1980s by proclamation of the Weinberger-Powell Doctrine, which boils down to an elaborate intellectual excuse for not using force at all except in the most favorable strategic, operational, and domestic political circumstances. Reinforced by the Defense Reorganization Act of 1986, which increased the weight and quality of military advice to civilian authority, the Weinberger-Powell Doctrine remains popular within the Pentagon and among both Republican and Democratic foreign policy minimalists on Capitol Hill.

---

[8]. See the author's *Perils of Reasoning by Historical Analogy, Munich, Vietnam, and American Use of Force Since 1945*. Occasional Paper No. 4 (Maxwell AFB, AL: Center for Strategy and Technology, Air War College, March 1998).

The taproot of the Vietnam Syndrome as it has evolved since the war is the present political and military elites' conviction that the public has no stomach for casualties, and therefore that use of force in situations of optional intervention should be prepared to sacrifice even operational effectiveness for the sake of casualty avoidance. This conviction produced almost a decade of American strategic fecklessness in the former Yugoslavia, culminating in a NATO war against Serbia in which force protection was accorded priority over mission accomplishment. The result: a bizarre disconnect between political ends and military means in which an exclusive and initially timid deployment of air power quickly provoked an acceleration of the very Serbian ethnic cleansing of Kosovo that formed NATO's immediate causus belli.

Consider the joint testimony of Secretary of Defense William Cohen and Chairman of the Joint Chiefs of Staff Gen. Henry Shelton: "the paramount lesson learned from Operation Allied Force is that the well-being of our people must remain our first priority."[9] If indeed this was the premier lesson, then U.S. troops should never be exposed to combat in the first place. They should be kept at home—better yet, demobilized. Or, at a minimum, as in Operation Allied Force, policy makers should confine America's enemies to those incapable of shooting back in the air while simultaneously offering those enemies nothing to shoot at on the ground. Consider also the postwar caution of NATO's then Supreme Allied Commander, General Wesley

---

[9]. Secretary of Defense William S. Cohen and General Henry H. Shelton, Chairman of the Joint Chiefs of Staff, "Joint Statement on Kosovo After Action Review," before the Senate Armed Services Committee, October 14, 1999, p. 27.

Clark: "in an air campaign you don't want to lose aircraft because when you start to lose these expensive machines the countdown starts against you. The headlines begin to shout, 'NATO loses a second aircraft,' and the people ask, 'How long can this go on?' "[10]

The presumption of public casualty intolerance—regardless of circumstances except for wars of national survival—prompts use-of-force aversion. It also removes force as a tool of coercive diplomacy, undermines the military ethic of self-sacrifice and mission accomplishment, disconcerts allies, emboldens enemies, and puts at risk foreigners who seek America's protection. To be sure, it was Serbian thugs who victimized the Albanian Kosovars, but the latter were also victimized, if indirectly, by NATO's casualty phobia.[11]

Indeed, casualty phobia reflects a perhaps willfully misperceived lesson of the Vietnam War that is unfortunately shared by the present U.S. political and military leadership. The lesson of Vietnam is not the public's absolute intolerance of casualties, but rather that the American people's level of tolerance hinges on such reasonable criteria as perceived strength of interests at stake and on visible progress, or lack thereof, toward a

---

[10]. Wesley K. Clark, "The United States and NATO; The Way Ahead," *Parameters* (Winter1999-2000), pp. 8-9.

[11]. To be sure, Milosevic was always in a position to accelerate Kosovo's ethnic cleaning more quickly than NATO could put in place opposite Serbia a ground combat force option capable of stopping it. However, an early attempt to put one in place might have conveyed sufficient seriousness of intent to deter Operation Horseshoe. It could not possibly have been less discouraging that President Clinton's public renunciation of a NATO ground force option.

satisfactory resolution of hostilities. "There is no clear evidence that Americans will not tolerate many body bags in the course of intervention where vital interests are not at stake," observes Richard K. Betts. "What is crucial for maintaining public support is not [the incursion of] casualties per se, but casualties in an *inconclusive* war, casualties that the public sees as being suffered indefinitely, for no clear, good, or achievable purpose."[12] The contingent nature of the public's casualty tolerance, heavily influenced by presidential leadership in mobilizing public opinion, is supported by study after study,[13] though such studies seem to make no impression upon the White House and Pentagon.

Indeed, presidential leadership and the conclusiveness of combat may be more important determinants of public tolerance of casualties than the presence of vital strategic interests (the definition of which is also mightily subject to presidential influence). Certainly, no such interests were present in Grenada in 1983, yet the quick and conclusive U.S. invasion of that island and overthrow of its Cuban-supported

---

[12]. Richard K. Betts, "What Will It Take to Deter the United States?", *Parameters* (Winter 1995-96), p. 76. Also see Andrew P.N. Erdmann, "The U.S. Presumption of Quick, Costless Wars," *Orbis* (Summer 1999), pp. 363-381.

[13]. See, for example, the following studies performed by the Rand Corporation of Santa Monica, California: Mark Lorrell and Charles Kelley, Jr., *Casualties, Public Opinion, and Presidential Policy During the Vietnam War*, 1985; Benjamin C. Schwarz, *Casualties, Public Opinion, and U.S. Military Intervention, Implications for U.S. Regional Deterrence Strategies*, 1994; and Eric V. Larson *Casualties and Consensus, The Historical Role of Casualties in Domestic Support for U.S. Military Operations*, 1996.

Marxist government was cheered by a majority of Americans. Even Iraq's invasion of Kuwait in 1990 posed no direct threat to the security of the United States, and President Bush initially had difficulty in mobilizing public and congressional support for his decision to force the Iraqis out of Kuwait one way or the other. But in the end he did so (though by only a five-vote margin in the Senate), leading the country into a war for which the public's expectation of casualties turned out to be much higher than the number actually incurred.[14]

Recent comprehensive polling data and other information marshaled by the Triangle Institute for Security Studies' Project on the Gap Between the Military and Civilian Society confirms not only that "the strong belief of civilian and military elites that the American public will not support casualties is not supported by the survey data," but also that the "mass public says that it will accept casualties" in such scenarios as defending Taiwan and stopping Iraq from acquiring weapons of mass destruction.[15] The data further reveals that civilian policy

---

[14]. Though U.S. casualties were miraculously low (146 killed in action, over a third by friendly fire), both the public and Capitol Hill were prepared to accept a much higher toll. Operation Desert Storm was planned by the Pentagon and authorized by the President on the assumption that American war dead might number in the thousands. See Erdmann, op. cit., pp. 375-376; and John Mueller, *Policy and Opinion in the Gulf War* (Chicago: University of Chicago Press, 1994), pp. 45, 124, 306-307.

[15]. Digest of Findings and Studies Presented to the Conference on the Military and Civilian Society, Catigny Conference Center, 1st Division Museum, 28-29 October 1999. http//www.unc.edu/depts/tiss/CIVMIL.htm, p. 5.

makers, and even more so senior military officers, are much more casualty intolerant than the average American citizen.[16]

Elite casualty phobia is thus real, but it also may be self-serving. The assumption of public casualty intolerance excuses presidents and generals alike from taking the kind of battlefield risks that might invite casualties, even though the price may be mission frustration or failure. Indeed, casualty phobia has become an important ally of the Weinberger-Powell Doctrine: both serve, albeit less than perfectly, as self-deterrents to military action altogether, or, at least to risky military action, in circumstances not involving manifest threats to core U.S. security interests.

The strategic consequences of elite casualty phobia as well as its implications for the military ethic have been treated elsewhere.[17] Suffice to say here that they are averse and include: political vacillation in war-threatening crises, degraded military effectiveness, lowered deterrence, discouraged friends

---

[16]. Peter D. Feaver and Christopher Gelpi, "How Many Deaths are Acceptable? A Surprising Answer," *Washington Post*, November 7, 1999.

[17]. See, for example, Edward N. Luttwak, "Where Are the Great Powers?", *Foreign Affairs* (July/August 1994), pp. 23-28; James Nathan, "The Rise and Decline of Coercive Statecraft," *Proceedings* (October 1995), pp. 59-65; Mark J. Conversino, "Sawdust Superpower: The Perceptions of U.S. Casualty Tolerance in the Post-Gulf War Era," *Strategic Review* (Winter 1997), pp. 15-23; and Karl P. Mueller, "Politics, Death, and Morality in U.S. Foreign Policy" and Charles K. Hyde, "Casualty Aversion: Implications for Policy Makers and Senior Military Officers," *Aerospace Power Journal* (Summer 2000), pp. 12-16 and 17-27, respectively.

and allies, and a morally compromised professional military ethos—and above all politically inconclusive uses of force. In the short run it is always less risky to treat the symptoms of aggression rather than its political sources. Yet casualty phobia encourages strategically indecisive, even half-baked, uses of force. A refusal to take advantage of the opportunity of war to use the force necessary to topple the regimes of Saddam Hussein and Slobodan Milosevic, both of whom senior American policy makers publicly compared to Adolph Hitler, simply invited more war later. To be sure, in both the Gulf War and the War Over Kosovo, U.S. political objectives were limited, and did not include enemy regime overthrow. Yet, surely, the exclusion of regime change was driven mainly by fear of the anticipated risks and costs involved.

None of this is to suggest that commanders should not do everything in their power to avoid unnecessary casualties, but the standard of judging the difference between necessary and unnecessary must be mission accomplishment. There is wide ground between the recklessness of a George Armstrong Custer and the timidity of a George Brinton McClellan. Custer placed his own celebrity above the lives of his men, whereas McClellan placed risk avoidance ahead of mission accomplishment. The better model ought to be a Winfield Scott or a Matthew Ridgway.

IV. IMPLICATIONS FOR FORCE STRUCTURE AND TECHNOLOGY CHOICES

The displacement of large-scale inter-state conventional warfare by smaller, largely intra-state warfare argues strongly for abandonment of the two-major-theater-wars planning construct and greater investment in forces more suitable for the kinds of small wars and peace-enforcement enterprises that have come to dominate the Pentagon's operational agenda since the end of the Cold War. Excessive casualty aversion argues equally strongly for increased investment in air power, stand-off precision-guided munitions, and space power.

It is the duty of force planners to respond to change in both the international and domestic political arenas. It is not their duty to insist that change conform to existing force structure and past technology choices, or to delude themselves into believing that mastery of conventional warfare provides sufficient military protection of U.S. strategic interests. Yet the construct of two simultaneous major theater wars based on past wars in Korea and the Persian Gulf is an apparition that hinders sound thought about, and ultimately American military effectiveness in, the post-Cold War international political environment. To be sure, one can conjure up all sorts of wars in all sorts of places,[18] and it would be foolish to ignore completely the possibility of getting stuck in two of them at the same time, as the United States once did from 1941 to 1945.

But the scenario of the post-Cold War U.S. military being called upon to wage two big conventional wars at the same time speaks more to the internal budgetary and bureaucratic interests of the armed forces than it does to the radically altered external strategic environment. The scenario's main function has always been to offer a construct to preserve as much Cold War conventional force structure as possible during

---

[18]. In a 1984 professional conference, the author was berated by a noted defense policy analyst for dismissing the Bering Strait as a likely avenue of a Soviet invasion of the continental United States. More recently, he learned from a colleague that a hostile India will emerge as America's next great strategic rival.

a period of inevitable cuts. The view of the National Defense Panel of 1997 is correct: the two-war scenario is "a force-sizing function and not a strategy. We are concerned that this construct may have become a force-protection mechanism—a means of justifying the current force structure—especially for those searching for the certainties of the Cold War era."[19]

The scenario is also, however, historically most improbable. Furthermore, it ignores the changing state of the military balance in the Persian Gulf and on the Korean Peninsula as well as recent political developments in both Koreas.

On the matter of historical improbability, it is first necessary to concede that during the Second World War the United States did indeed find itself fighting what amounted to two separate major wars, one against Germany in Europe and the other against Japan in the Pacific. But the circumstances of U.S. entry into World War II were strategically extraordinary, therefore most unlikely ever to be repeated.[20] The two-war construct is simply no longer intellectually viable *within the realm of reasonably acceptable strategic risk.* At no time during the twelve years of the Korean War, the Vietnam War, and the Gulf crisis of 1990-1991 did another adversary with whom the

---

[19]. *Transforming Defense, National Security in the 21st Century*, Report of the National Defense Panel, December 1997, pp. 23-24.

[20]. The Japanese attack on Pearl Harbor on December 7, 1941, and Hitler's utterly gratuitous declared of war on the United States four days later proved to be strategic disasters for both Tokyo and Berlin. This was hardly the first or last time the United States faced a strategically incompetent adversary, but it was the only time it faced two of them simultaneously.

United States was not at war choose challenge to the United States militarily. States almost always go to war for reasons specific in time and place, and only rarely simply because an adversary happens to be at war with another state.

The two-war scenario is being kept alive because the armed services need it to validate existing force structure and because the State Department doesn't want to take the diplomatic heat of a one-war construct, which would imply, among other things, that if the United States was already at war in the Persian Gulf, it would not come to the assistance of Seoul if South Korea was attacked. The two-war scenario helps inside the Beltway, but it hinders those outside Washington who must implement the strategy.

Moreover, one cannot even speak of a conventional military balance any longer in the Persian Gulf. There is little hostile power on the northern side left for American might to balance. Revolution, war, and international isolation destroyed Iran's capacity to project conventional military power beyond its borders, and the Gulf War crippled Iraq's once vaunted army. Even the State Department has demoted Iraq, Iran (and North Korea) from "rogue states" to "states of concern."

As for North Korea, it operates in an exceptionally unfavorable strategic environment. Its superpower patron has disappeared, its economy has all but failed, its military is obsolete, and it faces a much more powerful South Korea backed by a credible U.S. military guarantee. War would be suicide for the North's communist regime, and there is no reason to believe that the North Korean leadership is blind to this reality. Estimates of war's probability on the Peninsula must also take into account political change, and here the news is even better. Significant leadership change has taken place in both Seoul and Pyongyang, resulting in a publicly convivial face-to-face meeting between the two heads of state that would have been unthinkable just a couple of years ago. The meeting did not, of course, remove the mighty obstacles to Korea's reunification, but the beginning of a direct political dialogue between Seoul and Pyongyang surely reduces the chances of war.

The two-war construct could be replaced by a one-war-plus standard, the "plus" being one or more of what the Pentagon now terms "small scale contingencies," the most demanding of which would be small wars like the war against Serbia and such peace-enforcement operations as those now being performed in Bosnia and Kosovo. The United States has never been prepared to fund the forces necessary to do justice to a realistic two-war scenario since it was first postulated in the mistitled 1993 *Bottom-Up Review*. This ends/means gap has been the biggest open defense secret in Washington.[21] A potential added advantage of moving to a one-plus standard would be moving the defense debate off the mantra of force size to that of force composition.

Indeed, effective policing of failed states requires forces dedicated to that mission. Peace enforcement is as different from "real" war as are special operations, for which the United States retains dedicated forces under a separate command. To

---

[21]. The author has participated in several war games in recent years designed to test the capacity of extant forces to handle two overlapping wars in the Persian Gulf and Northeast Asia. In each case, shortages in airlift, bombers, stand-off precision munitions and other critical items were offset by rigged and often unrealistic turns of events postulated by game controllers.

be sure, existing U.S. conventional forces already bring much to the peace enforcement table. Among the items they can and have provided are logistics support, transport, communications, and surveillance. And in the case of such things as major evacuations and enforcing "no-fly" zones, only conventional forces can do the job. Yet, conventional ground forces and operational/tactical doctrines are not suitable for peace enforcement operations. The starting point rules of engagement for such operations—as it is for counter-insurgency operations—is the imperative of utmost restraint and discrimination in applying force. Firepower is an instrument of last rather than first resort. There is no big enemy to close with and destroy, but rather the presence of threatened civilian populations that must be protected in a way that minimizes collateral damage. Conventional ground force preparation for peace enforcement accordingly requires major doctrinal and training deprogramming of conventional military habits and reprogramming with alien tactics, doctrine, and heavy political oversight of enforcement operations. Needless to say, forces so reprogrammed—commonly manpower intensive and relatively low firepower—will not be optimized for big, high-tech conventional conflicts. Peace enforcement operations require the patient performance of mostly non-heroic missions often under conditions of prolonged and severe stress. Satisfaction of a job well done hinges on dramatic events, such as resumption of hostilities, that *don't* happen, that *don't* make the headlines.

Richard K. Betts objects that dedicated forces are impractical because Congress would not likely tolerate creation of significant forces that would not be available for standard conventional military missions but would require increases in defense spending. Yet Betts concedes that the only alternatives would be to minimize U.S. commitments to peace enforcement operations or accept the higher risk that other missions make come up short.[22] Moreover, there is no way to determine the level of future U.S. involvement in peace operations, which will be decided in part by a combination of presidential preference and the pressure of external events and other actors. The United States is also entering the strange new world of huge federal budget surpluses, which opens up the possibility of larger defense budgets.

The post-Cold War era of small, mostly intra-state wars also suggests the need for a new look at the distribution of heavy, medium, and light combat forces within the Army. Army Chief of Staff Eric K. Shinseki has already initiated just such an assessment, though the direction in which he is headed has not been greeted with enthusiasm by the armor and artillery communities. The idea is to create "medium" forces that are much more quickly deployable than heavy units but have significantly greater firepower than light forces. An interim force of up to eight brigades will be organized around off-the-shelf armored fighting vehicles weighing no more than 20 tons (compared to the 60-70-ton Abrams tank) and mounting new technology guns of smaller than current tank caliber but of equal lethality. Each brigade, which would be carved out of existing Army force structure—largely at the expense of heavy

---

[22]. Richard K. Betts, *Military Readiness, Concepts, Choices, Consequences* (Washington, D.C.: Brookings Institution, 1995), pp. 202-204.

divisions—would be deployable by air anywhere overseas in 96 hours, and a medium division within 120 hours.[23]

During the war against Serbia, the Army was embarrassed by its strategic immobility, epitomized by the fiasco of Task Force Hawk, which consumed five tons for each of the 6,200 troops deployed (300 C-17 sorties).[24] Gen. Shinseki sees medium forces as a solution. His bold force structure initiative moves the Army away not only from the Cold War but also from a decade of self-congratulation over the Gulf War, which undoubtedly accounts in part for the considerable internal resistance of the "heavies" (the Army's armor and artillery "unions") to the creation of medium forces. Gen. Shinseki originally envisaged a medium force of up to five divisions, all

---

[23]. See "Highlights of the AUSA's Annual Meeting," *Army* (December 1999), pp. 45-52; Edward B. Atkeson, "Main Battle Tanks, To be or Not to be?", *Army* (January 2000), pp. 37-40; Scott R. Gourley, "New Brigade Structure Begins to Emerge," *Army* (February 2000), pp. 33-34; Scott R. Gourley, "The Army Stages a Kentucky Demo to Define 'the Art of the Possible'," *Army* (March 2000), pp. 20-26; Jason Sherman, "Dream Work," *Armed Forces Journal International* (May 2000), pp. 25-28; Daniel L. Whiteside, "Slow Down!", *Armed Forces Journal International* (May 2000), pp. 30-33; Mark J. O'Konski, "Enhancing Army Deployability," *Army* (May 2000), pp. 29-31; and Theodore G. Stroup, Jr., "The Ongoing Army Transformation," *Army* (July 2000), pp. 7-10.

[24]. Dana Priest, "Army's Apache Helicopter Rendered Impotent," *Washington Post*, December 29, 1999; Sean D. Naylor, "Apache Task Force Deploys to Albania," *Army Times*, April 19, 1999, p. 8; Sean D. Naylor, "On Our Way to Hell," *Army Times*; May 3, 1999, p. 10; and Matthew Cox, "Troops and Tanks Beef Up Task Force Hawk," *Army Times*, May 10, 1999, p. 14.

based on wheeled rather than tracked vehicles.[25] But he has had to settle for no more than eight brigades and a reopening of the issue of wheeled v. tracked vehicles. Too, Gen. Shinseki may be retired before his already reduced medium force initiative fully "takes" within the Army.

Medium forces as envisaged by Gen. Shinseki might indeed have been usable with considerable effectiveness in the war against Serbia. But President Clinton's prior political decision to exclude employment of any ground forces presumably would have included even strategically mobile medium forces. However, the unavailability of such forces may have reinforced his decision, and future presidents in different overseas crises might use them if they were available.

Indeed, the war against Serbia revealed the Army to be the chief loser to elite casualty phobia. Commitment of ground forces conveys greater seriousness of political resolve than commitment of air and sea forces precisely because ground forces are the most manpower intensive and therefore the greatest source of casualties. The chief beneficiary of casualty phobia predictably has been air power in general and the Air Force in particular. For all the talk of "jointness" since passage of Goldwater-Nichols, presidents in the post-Cold War world of small wars have increasingly embraced air power as a *substitute* for ground power. Thus the emerging predilection for cruise missiles over manned aircraft, and manned aircraft over anything on the ground—a predilection greatly reinforced by air power's single-handed victory in the war against Serbia at no cost in Americans killed in action. The U.S. Army was excluded

---

[25]. "Highlights of AUSA's Meeting," op. cit., p. 49.

altogether from combat, performing instead the *post*war mission of peace enforcement.

Even when Iraq challenged concrete U.S. strategic interests in the Persian Gulf a decade ago, Operation Desert Storm was crafted and conducted with casualty minimization as the first order of business. In fact, AirLand Battle was effectively disassembled into a sequential air campaign followed by a short ground war, with most of the air war serving as a gigantic artillery "prep" of Iraqi ground forces. The Army swept up Iraqi crockery smashed largely by air power.[26]

The argument here is not that the United States can or should rely from now on primarily, even exclusively, upon air power to do its military business; rather it is that *the political attractiveness of air power to a casualty-phobic national leadership is likely to reduce National Command Authority consideration of ground combat options in a crisis.* This will be true especially in small-war circumstances, which rarely include the presence of first-order strategic interests.

Admittedly, an air-option-only approach to dealing with small wars would be a mistake. Aside from conveying reluctance of political will to adversaries and allies alike, the military effectiveness of such an approach would be inherently circumscribed by air power's own limitations. Air power's record as a tool of political coercion is not impressive in the

---

[26]. This is certainly not to belittle the Army's and the Marine Corps' contribution to final victory. For Saddam Hussein, ground combat and the taking of territory is what war is all about, and it is more than coincidental that he ordered Kuwait's evacuation only after Coalition ground forces had—unexpectedly to him—entered Iraqi territory.

absence of other factors at play,[27] including the presence of ground forces. And as the war against Serbia demonstrated, air power can influence but not control events on the ground. Withholding ground forces simply because of fear of casualties renders the United States a one-armed superpower. It also reduces air power's potential effectiveness because the very presence of U.S. ground forces, even if not actually committed to combat, forces the enemy to concentrate his ground forces, thereby increasing their vulnerability to air attack.

Nonetheless, if the present level of casualty phobia persists among U.S. political and military elites, then those elites have an obligation to shift defense dollars away from ground power and toward air power. What is the point of continuing to maintain the present level of investment in strategically sluggish heavy ground forces in an era of markedly declining prospects for large-scale conventional wars involving the United States and of declining political will to place ground forces in general in harm's way? This is not an Army v. Air Force issue; the U.S. Navy's surface fleet is organized primarily around air power, and

---

[27]. The War Over Kosovo is a case in point. Obviously, Milosevic would not have quit absent the bombing. Yet other factors of unknown relative importance were also at play: a softening of NATO's original settlement terms; Russia's diplomatic defection to the G-7 war termination position; indications that NATO was moving toward a ground combat option; and increased Kosovo Liberation Army activity on the ground. The coercive success of Operation Deliberate Force's 1995 air strikes against Bosnian-Serb targets in Bosnia also must be seen in the context of other events, including Bosnian Serb defeat on the ground by Croatian and Bosnia Muslim forces, and Milosevic's decision to cease Belgrade's military and diplomatic support of the Bosnian Serb government.

it made indispensable contributions to the air war against Serbia.

Precedent for a budgetary redistribution toward air power may be found in the 1950s. Whatever the weaknesses of the strategy of Massive Retaliation, the strategy represented a conscious decision by President Eisenhower to base the security of the United States on deterrence via the instrument of nuclear-armed air power. From this decision flowed a dramatic redirection of defense spending away from conventional military forces and into the nuclear and air power (especially long-range bombardment) accounts. By the late 1950s, almost half of the U.S. defense budget was going to the Air Force, which was dominated by the now-defunct Strategic Air Command.

The point is not whether Massive Retaliation was good or bad; rather, it is that the strategy had budgetary imperatives that Eisenhower recognized and acted upon. So too does the present national leadership's de facto embrace of an air-only-if-possible-and-still-air-mostly-if-not strategy in precisely the kind of small wars that have come to dominate the international political landscape. If, from here on, air power is going to do America's heavy military lifting with ground forces sitting along the sidelines, then the defense budget ought to reflect this new reality.

Within the air accounts, moreover, additional money should be moved into technologies that reduce air crew exposure to possible loss. This means investment in ever longer-range stand-off precision munitions, and, above all, in unmanned aerial vehicles (UAVs). The greater the precision, the smaller the munition required, and therefore the greater the reduction of impact on people and things not intentionally targeted.

Increased reliance on UAVs (which include cruise missiles) and on large stand-off platforms like the B-2 may encounter resistance among the so-called "fighter mafia" which dominates the Air Force leadership. Pilotless vehicles are just that, and the leadership values acquisition of the F-22 above all else, including a reopening of the B-2 production line and creation of precision munitions stocks on hand sufficient to preclude the risk of encountering wartime shortages (as was the case in the War Over Kosovo). Yet UAVs and the B-2 satisfy the imperatives of elite casualty phobia. Both are difficult to target; the UAVs in any event don't have aircrew; and while B-2s do, the ratio of crew to capacity to deliver precision munitions swamps that of any "tactical" aircraft. During the war against Serbia, a total of 22 strategic bombers (6 B-2s, 6 B-1s, and 10 B-52s) accounted for over one-half (12,000 out of 23,000) bombs and missiles expended against Serbian targets.[28]

Of particular priority is the need for an autonomously-piloted vehicle. Such a vehicle has been advocated for years, but the technology required is still out of reach, as is even some of the science. A UAV that is remotely controlled has great limitations because the situational awareness of the "pilot," and to obtain that awareness would require a large data "pipe" that could be

---

[28]. Hans Mark, address before the Potomac Institute's Conference on "Out of the Box and Into the Future: A Dialogue Between Warfighters and Scientists on Far-Future Warfare (2025)," June 27, 2000, Washington, D.C. Conference proceedings soon to be available at www.potomacinstitute.org.

vulnerable and almost certainly would greatly increase the cost of the UAV. An autonomous vehicle solves these problems, yet introduces others because it would require a computer that could "think" and that would be asked to make life-and-death decisions on the battlefield. These are not insurmountable challenges, but they demand increased funding.

Investment in the search for effective non-lethal technologies also needs acceleration, in part because dual-use targets are becoming increasingly important objects of air power's employment as a tool of coercive diplomacy. "Brute force" bombs and missiles are fine for blowing up big fixed targets and large enemy forces out in the open, but they are not optimized to take down power grids, "fry" electronics, and "zap" communications in a manner that minimizes collateral damage. Here, lasers can play a role, but high-powered microwave systems hold the best promise because their dial-a-yield allows them to be tailored to a particular target.

Finally, there is the issue of space. Space has become inseparable from air power, and it reinforces air power's capacity to minimize friendly military and enemy civilian casualties. The question is whether space should continue to be kept weapon-free or integrated into the U.S. military's overall offensive and defensive capabilities. The very use of the term "aerospace" power suggests the answer.

In making decisions to use—or not use—military force, presidents must weigh considerations of both military effectiveness and domestic politics. The United States is, after all, a democracy, and, contrary to conventional wisdom, politics never stopped at the water's edge. Yet if perceived domestic political considerations become the enemy of military effectiveness, to the point of arbitrarily excluding use of one form of military power in its entirety—and this is the direction where America unfortunately seems to be headed in the present era of small wars in out-of-the-way places, then the United States must alter established force structure and patterns of defense spending to maximize the effectiveness of the forms of military power it *is* prepared to use.

It is clear that the ground force component can devise new and interesting approaches to mitigate the casualty issue and make itself a more relevant tool for presidents in this interregnum of relative peace.   The White House always needs as many politically usable military options in a crisis as it can get. For the moment, however, it is the air arm that offers the quickest and most viable solutions because of its intrinsic nature of being above the fight.

Editor's note: Two years after "Failed States and Casualty Phobia," Jeffrey Record returned to the topic with an essay titled "Collapsed Countries, Casualty Dread, and the New American Way of War." In this piece, Record expanded on earlier themes, proposing that "the combination of failed states, elite casualty phobia, and unfolding aerial precision strike and associated technologies is profoundly altering the locus and style of future US military interventions overseas. The United States is beginning to practice a new way of warfare in parts of the world peripheral to traditional American security interests."

In 2000, when Record's earlier piece appeared, his touchstones were the first Gulf War and the Balkans. In 2002, when "Collapsed Countries" appeared, Record could draw on

Afghanistan as well. He observed that "US combat operations in Afghanistan were nonetheless conducted in a manner consistent with those of casualty-phobic Operations Deliberate Force (Bosnia) and Allied Force (Kosovo). Either the political and military leadership remained casualty-phobic, or circumstances permitted a cheap victory, or—most probably—both."

Record reiterated that "Casualty dread is most acute among the military leadership, especially that of the Army, which is still in the grip of the Vietnam Syndrome."

The core of his new piece was to ask "Are we looking at a new way of war? A way that allows the United States to prevail strategically at little risk to its own military forces? One that avoids (for Americans) the agony of danger and death?"

Record claimed not to be resisting this new way of war. He wrote, "Rather, the argument is simply to recognize two important caveats in embracing the new way of war: first, that success may be critically dependent on the availability of competent local surrogates with their own political agendas; and second, that the character of the new way of war could transform our very approach to the use of force."

These lines appear as true after the Iraq experience as before.

"Collapsed Countries" appeared in the Army War College Magazine *Parameters*. It evoked a critical letter and a response from Record, both being of general interest on these topics.

To the Editor:

The article "Collapsed Countries, Casualty Dread, and the New American Way of War" (Parameters, Summer 2002) by Jeffrey Record should be thought-provoking for those concerned with the future role of the Army in national defense and its force structure. Although well organized, the article demonstrates the corruption of logic employed by air-centric strategists to gain a priority role for airpower and relegate land forces to small units of marginal relevance.

First, the first section heading, "Failed States as the Primary Threat," is an apt title for the air-centric argument that goes something like this: The employment of military means since Desert Storm (e.g. Bosnia, Kosovo, Afghanistan, etc.) has been primarily precision-strike missiles and aircraft with small, light "scouts" (as the author calls them) on the ground; therefore, we should orient our entire defense organization to handle this type of operation. The author supports this argument with a mantra that failed states are the "primary source" of instability in the world. This thought process is flawed because the frequency of use of one type of military capability should not be the sole, nor even the dominant, factor for structuring our armed forces. This logic ignores the very real, more dangerous threats in the world today that require conventional ground forces, including the heavy component of conventional forces (Korea, Iraq, China, etc.). The fact such threats have remained relatively inactive the last decade shows the value of having conventional forces in our arsenal. Does anyone think that Saddam Hussein would hesitate to reinvade Kuwait, or even Saudi Arabia, if we do away with our current land force capability? We must organize our military with priority given to the most dangerous threats, even if the frequency with which they occur is lower than the Kosovo-type intervention.

The author looks at the recent application of military power with blinders, looking only at US operations. Other military forces in the world, taking a wider view of recent history, seem to disagree with him. Note Israel's recent incursions into Palestine (perhaps a failed state even under the author's definition?) with tanks, armored personnel carriers, and mechanized infantry as the weapons of choice. How would the author propose to carry out a similar operation with an air-centric force? The current face-off between India and Pakistan adds another contrary example not mentioned by Record.

Second, the air-centric logic in the article also assumes the potential threat array will remain basically the same. This is a false assumption. How fast things can change. In 1986, no one would have predicted the military would have to prosecute Desert Storm a mere five years later. Leaders were frantic to "go light" then, just as they are now. Threats that require the use of conventional military ground power can grow and mature just as quickly as those requiring airpower alone. The timeline necessary to develop competent conventional ground power is much longer than the timeline for a conventional forces threat to emerge.

Third, the argument in the article uses distorted history to make the case for a future military consisting primarily of missiles, aircraft, and ground-based air control parties. The author apparently concurs with the opinion he quotes that the Gulf War, fought with conventional ground forces, was a "radically incomplete victory." According to the author, airpower "had already beaten" frontline Iraqi combat troops before the ground war commenced, ground combat units merely "chased" the few surviving Iraqi units off, and air was the "dominant arm of victory." These statements are simply untrue, as anyone in VII Corps, XVIII Airborne Corps, or the Tiger Brigade can attest.

In actual fact, the air war against Iraq was not operationally decisive—it did not force Saddam to move out of Kuwait, and it showed no potential for doing so even if we had gone on to bomb Iraqi forces for a year. It took conventional ground forces—a half million of them—and thousands of armored fighting vehicles to accomplish our operational goal, which we did, completely. And, there seems to be little doubt the airpower-claimed "body count" from the Gulf War was highly inflated.

On the other hand, Record argues, the Kosovo operation was a complete success. Air bombardment had "decisive strategic effects" and it, alone, created a "clear strategic win." This would be news to the thousands of Kosovar people killed and maimed when our airpower failed to stop a third-rate country from completing its ethnic cleansing. One must consider the question of how much capability we really have through airpower when, after two months of using our most capable air warfare systems, Milosevic was still thumbing his nose at us.

This last point drives home the Achilles' heel of air-centric logic. Airpower alone, even in the most favorable environment (such as Afghanistan) only has the capability for point destruction. This results in dispersal, not annihilation at the operational level. Airpower does not have the capability to "trap" enemy ground forces. This usually precludes a complete victory (witness the escape of bin Laden and Omar and hundreds if not thousands of Taliban fighters). Compare the results in Afghanistan in this regard with our operations in Panama, where Noriega and his cronies were trapped and captured quickly by ground forces. Airpower alone does not have the capability to "block" enemy ground forces. If it could not keep Milosevic from driving tens of thousands of people in front of him for the better part of two months, would it be able to prevent North Korean forces from seizing South Korea? Last, airpower alone does not have the capability to seize or hold ground, which is usually the main issue when it comes to our vital strategic interests.

I am glad Parameters saw fit to publish the article, as debate on this topic is critical. For it is through serious, reasoned debate that the flaws in the author's argument are exposed. Let us not find our sons and daughters who happen to join the Army or Marine Corps going off to war in ten years in some faraway land like Korea, Iraq, or larger countries on the Pacific Rim armed only with a rifle, a HUMMWV, and a UHF radio. We have a solemn obligation not to leave them holding the bag after our decisions on force structure.

Colonel Kris P. Thompson
Commander, 223d Infantry Regiment
California Army National Guard

To the Editor:

I read with great interest Jeffrey Record's thought-provoking article, "Collapsed Countries, Casualty Dread, and the New American Way of War." However, I believe the article incorrectly identifies the problem of casualty aversion as peculiar to American leaders because of their history and culture. In fact, casualty aversion is part of a broader phenomenon associated with democratic governments: namely, the need to maintain the consent and support so indispensable for winning wars.

Readers interested in this topic can explore it further in a carefully researched book by Dan Reiter and Allan C. Stam, *Democracies at War* (Princeton University Press, 2002). Drawing on data from the Correlates of War Project at the University of Michigan and the Historical Evaluation and Research Organization under contract for the US Army Concepts Analysis Agency, the authors conclude that since 1815 democracies have won more than three-quarters of the wars they have participated in. One aspect that explains the propensity of democracies to win wars is that they are better than autocratic states at initiating only those wars they are likely to win. The more prudent choices for initiating wars in turn are linked to the fact that democratic leaders are constrained to consider public opinion because such leaders can be voted out of office for failure. Concerns for retention of power thus induce leaders in a democracy to avoid starting risky wars. A related finding is that the propensity of democracies to win declines over time as a war drags on, presumably because of mounting casualties. In contrast, autocratic states have less of a probability of winning a war early, but their probability of winning does not decrease significantly as time passes. In other words, there is a natural tendency for leaders in any democracy to be casualty-averse.

Does this analysis then suggest that democracies are inherently at a disadvantage in any protracted conflict and that enemies need only to find a way to prolong the conflict and wait out a democracy? Not always, because although democracy has some disadvantage in a protracted war related to the danger of declining public support, a second factor may offset the disadvantage: The authors also suggest that democracies are better at warfighting than are non-democracies. Democratic political culture, placing an emphasis on rights and prerogatives, seems to carry over to the battlefield and leads to a higher level of initiative and innovation that proves indispensable for adaptation in a fluid battlefield environment. Thus, while a protracted conflict may offer some advantage to an autocratic state fighting a democracy, the autocratic state remains at a competitive disadvantage from the standpoint of warfighting.

Casualty aversion may only appear to look peculiarly American or more pronounced today because the United States is the most visible leader in the international system. In addition, both the withdrawal from Somalia and the war in Kosovo took place during the Clinton Administration and may reflect a greater level of casualty aversion associated with President Clinton and his Administration. One cannot necessarily extrapolate a trend that may not hold with subsequent administrations. To be sure, groups like the bin Laden network may have developed their strategies based on an assumption of US casualty aversion, but that does not necessarily mean the United States should develop its own military strategy relying predominantly on airpower.

If the real threat facing the United States derives from the phenomenon of failed states, the solution is not to rely on airpower to coerce without casualties in order to "overthrow" the failed states. Rather, the United States has the imperative for developing a multi-pronged approach that will assist with the creation of stable, decent political rule in these failed states.

Given the nature of the long-term problem, airpower has little role to play. And as far as relying on coercion to attain political objectives on the periphery, we would do well to recall a point made by Robert McNamara in his confessional on Vietnam, *In Retrospect: The Tragedy and Lessons of Vietnam*: "There may be a limit beyond which many Americans and much of the world will not permit the United States to go. The picture of the world's greatest superpower killing or seriously injuring 1,000 noncombatants a week while trying to pound a tiny backward nation into submission on an issue whose merits are hotly disputed, is not a pretty one."

Using airpower to avoid US casualties as a means to retain democratic support could well have the ironic effect of subverting that democratic consent because of a general revulsion against the brutality and disproportion of airpower applied for limited political purposes.

Janeen Klinger
Associate Professor of National Security
Command and Staff College, Marine Corps University
Quantico, Virginia

The Author Replies:

Colonel Thompson's commentary exemplifies the Army's understandable sensitivity to the issue of the continued utility of Cold War legacy conventional ground forces, especially heavy ground forces. I know of no one, including myself, who favors the elimination of such forces. My focus on the recent US airpower-centric wars in failed states was not an argument for doing away with armored forces and lots of boots on the ground. Rather, it reflected the combination of international political, domestic political, and technological change that has fundamentally altered where, how, and against whom we have fought and continue to fight in the post-Soviet era.

We do, however, seem to be running low on plausible scenarios involving massive and sustained US ground force combat. Colonel Thompson mentions North Korea, Iraq, China—and the example of Israeli armor on the West Bank. The United States, however, worries less about the obsolete North Korean and Iraqi armies than it does about Pyongyang's and Baghdad's missiles and weapons of mass destruction. Conventional deterrence has worked against both rogue states since 1991, and there is good reason to believe it will continue to do so unless, of course, the United States attacks those countries under the rubric of the Bush Doctrine. A US-Chinese war over Taiwan or the South China Sea would be largely an air and naval fight, unless the United States violated its long-standing and Vietnam War-reinforced strategic injunction of avoiding large wars on the Asian mainland. As for Israeli armor on the West Bank, I don't propose carrying out a similar operation anywhere. Americans are not in the business of conquest and repression of other peoples.

I share Colonel Thompson's view that the air war against Iraq was not operationally decisive; large and heavy US ground forces were indeed required to expel the Iraqi army from Kuwait. But were those forces themselves operationally decisive? Was not a key operational objective the destruction of the Republican Guard, and did not much of it escape through the Basra gate General Schwarzkopf mistakenly thought he had closed? Enough to keep Saddam Hussein in power and rob Operation Desert Storm of its strategic decisiveness?

Colonel Thompson also rightly points to the disconnect in Operation Allied Force between the military instrument selected—airpower—and the political objective it was designed to achieve—halting Milosevic's ethnic cleansing of Kosovo. The air campaign actually sparked an acceleration of Milosevic's war on Kosovar Albanians. The Clinton Administration's public renunciation of the ground force option was a monumental act of moral cowardice and strategic incompetence. Yet, in the end, airpower coerced Milosevic into abandoning Kosovo, where today NATO, not Serbian, boots are on the ground. Getting to that clear strategic win was not a pretty sight, but a clear strategic win it was.

As for the inherent limitations of airpower, I acknowledged them at the end of my article: The "conquest, occupation, and administration of territory . . . require 'boots on the ground' in sizable numbers. . . . Airpower's utility is also limited in peace enforcement operations, which require dedicated ground forces." I also condemned US air occupation zones in Iraq as having "done little to retard undesirable developments on the ground."

Janeen Klinger's commentary addresses my discussion of the fact and consequences of casualty phobia among American political and military elites. She uses the term "aversion," which refers to a healthy desire on the part of leaders of democratic societies to minimize casualties consistent with the achievement of wartime military missions. I use the term "phobia" to refer to a much more extreme phenomenon: a fear of casualties so overpowering as to induce the placement of the safety of the military instrument above the mission it is designed to accomplish. It was this phobia that we saw on display in Bosnia, Kosovo, and at Tora Bora, and which encouraged Osama bin Laden, among others, to believe that the United States was a gutless giant, a sawdust Caesar.

Casualty aversion is part of a broader phenomenon associated with democratic governments because of the need to maintain the consent and support so indispensable for winning wars. But among the fighting democracies, elite casualty phobia is unique to the United States and has been much remarked-upon both in America and overseas by friend and foe alike since the end of the Vietnam War, and especially since the American debacle in Somalia.

I certainly share Janeen Klinger's admiration for Dan Reiter and Allan Stam's path-breaking and myth-shattering *Democracies at War*, as well as her belief in the imperative of promoting the political and economic reconstruction of post-regime change failed states. As for the disastrous McNamara and his pathetic book—don't get me started.

Jeffrey Record

Force-Protection Fetishism

Sources, Consequences, and (?) Solutions

Jeffrey Record

In the summer of 2000, the Aerospace Power Journal published this article by Jeffrey Record as part of an collection of pieces on the effects of casualty aversion.

From the publication's introduction:

> In this article, expanded from a commentary published in the March 2000 issue of US Naval Institute *Proceedings*, Dr. Record brings up the issue of casualty aversion as a negative symptom of the Vietnam conflict and the Weinberger-Powell Doctrine. He argues, with strong accusations, that the current casualty "phobia" among the military and political leadership is unwarranted—because it is not shared by the populace at large—and detrimental to America's military effectiveness, thus giving us a reason to consider greater reliance on local surrogates and perhaps a change in force structure.

Fetish: an object of unreasonably obsessive attention or regard

THE VIETNAM SYNDROME is alive and better than well. It was not "kicked" in the Gulf War, as a triumphant President George Bush claimed. On the contrary, it has metamorphosed into a force-protection fetishism that threatens to corrupt American statecraft in the post-cold-war era.

Force-protection fetishism was on full display during the Kosovo crisis of 1999. American behavior during that crisis reflected a desperate unwillingness to place satisfaction of US armed intervention's political objective ahead of the safety of its military instrument. Ground-combat options were self-denied. Airpower was kept at safe altitudes. Clausewitz was stood on his head.

The immediate effect was aerial activity that permitted the enemy to pursue and accelerate the very ethnic cleansing of Kosovo that Operation Allied Force had intended to halt. The long-term effect was to broadcast to friend and foe alike America's Achilles' heel as we enter the twenty-first century. For the peoples of the former Yugoslavia, the result was the political survival of Slobodan Milosevic, a two-bit Balkan Hitler, and the operational survival, virtually intact, of the Serbian army. Allied Force thus left the door open for Milosevic to start his fifth war (against Montenegro) in the Balkans. Was preserving the life of a single American pilot—a volunteer professional—worth jeopardizing the lives of 1,600,000 Kosovar Albanians and God-knows-how-many future victims of Serbian aggression?

Nor is force-protection fetishism a passing phenomenon. It derives from America's disastrous experience in Vietnam and prevails among the present national political and military elites, who may have wrongly convinced themselves that the American people have no stomach for casualties, regardless of the circumstances in which they are incurred. Indeed, for these elites, Vietnam is the great foreign-policy referent experience— one seemingly validated by failed US intervention in Lebanon and Somalia.

Force-protection fetishism corrupts the use of force because it ignores war as "a true political instrument, a continuation of political activity by other means."[29] Effective use of force rests on recognition of the intimate relationship between military means and political ends. Obsession with keeping the former out of harm's way, even at the expense of aborting attainment of the latter, violates war's very essence as an act of policy. Indeed, one should not make a decision to use force when force protection assumes greater importance than the political object on behalf of which one contemplates its employment. Yet, the United States proceeded to attack Serbia with the primary purpose of avoiding American casualties. Lack of loss—not mission accomplishment—became the standard for judging the success of Allied Force.

Consider the joint statement by Secretary of Defense William Cohen and Gen Henry Shelton, chairman of the Joint Chiefs of Staff (CJCS), that "the paramount lesson learned from Operation Allied Force is that the well-being of our people must remain our first priority."[30] Consider also the postwar caution of Gen Wesley Clark, supreme allied commander of the North Atlantic Treaty Organization (NATO): "In an air campaign you don't want to lose aircraft" because when "you start to lose these expensive machines the countdown starts against you. The

---

[29] Carl von Clausewitz, *On War*, ed. and trans. Michael Howard and Peter Paret (Princeton, N.J.: Princeton University Press, 1976), 87.
[30] Secretary of Defense William S. Cohen and Gen Henry Shelton, chairman of the Joint Chiefs of Staff, "Joint Statement on Kosovo After-Action Review," before the Senate Armed Services Committee, 14 October 1999, 27.

headlines begin to shout, 'NATO loses a second aircraft,' and the people ask, 'How long can this go on?' "[31]

One cannot imagine Henry Stimson, George S. Patton, or Curtis LeMay ever uttering such statements. Surely we must make a distinction between, on the one hand, the moral and political imperative of shielding military forces from risks that are superfluous to the accomplishment of operational and strategic objectives and, on the other hand, the subordination of those objectives to pursuit of the ideal of bringing every soldier home alive. Casualty-phobic timidity on the battlefield can be just as self-defeating as bloodthirsty recklessness. One Grant is worth a dozen McClellans and Custers. Should it have taken 78 days of bombing by the most powerful military alliance in history to convince Milosevic to accept NATO's watered-down terms for peace?

If protecting one's own troops is the greatest concern, then why expose them to combat at all? Keep them home. At the least, select only enemies incapable of fighting us in the air, as was the situation over Kosovo, and offer them nothing to shoot at on the ground as well. Indeed, why not do away with casualty-prone ground forces altogether and rely instead exclusively on airpower? Not to cast aspersions on our very capable surface forces, but think of the budgetary and force-structural implications of a US Army reduced to performing homeland defense tasks and burials at Arlington Cemetery!

During the cold war, the term half war referred to a war with enemies other than Russia and China. Perhaps it should now be

---

[31] Wesley K. Clark, "The United States and NATO: The Way Ahead," Parameters, Winter 1999–2000, 8–9

redefined to mean wars waged without the employment of US ground forces.

The Corrupting Agent: The Weinberger-Powell Doctrine

Force-protection fetishism is rooted in Vietnam—specifically in the resultant Weinberger-Powell Doctrine, which is the intellectual construct of the strategic lessons that many military professionals drew from the war. Caspar Weinberger, President Ronald Reagan's secretary of defense, proposed six "tests" for using force, later amended by Gen. Colin Powell's emphasis on overwhelming force. These tests effectively deny the legitimacy of force as a tool of coercive diplomacy by restricting its use to circumstances involving clear and present threats to manifestly vital national interests.[32] Such circumstances implicitly generate public and congressional support and place an explicit premium on overwhelming force to complete the job as quickly and cheaply as possible. Force is to be employed as a substitute for politics rather than its extension, which in turn strips diplomacy of any ability to coerce and thereby deter or alter adversarial behavior that could lead to war.

But is not force without war almost always preferable to war itself? Weinberger's tests included the presence of vital interests, a determination to win, the establishment of clear political and military objectives, the use of properly sized forces, an assurance of public and congressional support prior to

---

[32] Powell served as Weinberger's military aide and helped draft Weinberger's famous National Press Club speech entitled "The Uses of Military Power," delivered on 28 November 1984. Reprinted in Caspar Weinberger, Fighting for Peace: Seven Critical Years in the Pentagon (New York: Warner Books, 1990), 429–45.

involvement, and the exhaustion of all diplomatic alternatives prior to using force as a last resort. But the tests always raised more questions than they answered. What are vital interests, and who defines them? What does "winning" mean? Does not war impose its own dynamic influence on political and military objectives? How is assured public and congressional support to be gained in advance, to say nothing of maintained throughout hostilities? And are there not circumstances that encourage an early use of force rather than its employment as a last resort? Is this not the supreme lesson of Munich?

Ironically, adherence to the Weinberger-Powell Doctrine would likely have reinforced the democracies' appeasement of Hitler at Munich because an Anglo-French resort to war against Germany in October 1938 over Czechoslovakia's Sudetenland would have satisfied none of the doctrine's tests for using force. Even more ironically, this doctrine would have encouraged the United States to plunge into the Vietnam War. In 1965 the United States considered its vital interests at risk in Indochina and intervened as a last resort, an action that commanded widespread public, congressional, and editorial support. As for overwhelming force, neither the British nor the French in 1938 were in a position to conduct effective offensive military operations against Germany. In Vietnam, however, the United States ultimately brought to bear much greater firepower proportional to that of the Vietnamese communists than it did against Iraq in the Gulf.

The Weinberger-Powell Doctrine implicitly assumes that public tolerance of casualties is minimal in circumstances that do not satisfy the doctrine's use-of-force criteria, and this assumption elevates casualty minimization above mission accomplishment. Yet, this assumption not only runs afoul of substantial evidence to the contrary but also ignores the role of presidential leadership in shaping public opinion on behalf of using force. The assumption furthermore subverts the integrity of military intervention by compromising its potential operational and strategic effectiveness.

Public Opinion and Casualties

Casualty phobia reflects a misperceived lesson of the Vietnam War that, unfortunately, is shared among some senior political and military leaders. The lesson of Vietnam (and of Lebanon and Somalia) is not the public's absolute intolerance of casualties but an attitude toward casualties contingent on such reasonable criteria as perceived strength of interests at stake and progress toward a satisfactory resolution of hostilities. Casualties incurred in protracted, inconclusive wars waged for unconvincing goals are not the same as losses taken on behalf of decisive military operations launched for a compelling cause.[33] Americans will not accept the same blood risk to prevail in strategically inconsequential civil wars in Lebanon and Somalia that they willingly accepted in defeating Nazi Germany and containing the Soviet Union.

The public's casualty tolerance depends on circumstances that include not only presidential success or failure in mobilizing public opinion but also enemy behavior itself. The Japanese attack on Pearl Harbor instantly dissolved the America First movement as a domestic political obstacle to President Franklin Roosevelt's foreign policy, and the manifest personal and

---

[33] See Richard K. Betts, "What Will It Take to Deter the United States?" Parameters, Winter 1995–1996, 70–79. See also Andrew P. N. Erdmann, "The U.S. Presumption of Quick, Costless Wars," Orbis, Summer 1999, 363–81.

political evil of Saddam Hussein greatly facilitated George Bush's successful demonization of the Iraqi dictator. In contrast, not even the Great Communicator, Ronald Reagan, could explain to the American people exactly what US military intervention in Lebanon was all about; nor could Bill Clinton convey to the public and Congress a persuasive reason for invading Haiti. Unfortunately, although study after study supports the contingent nature of the public's tolerance of casualties,[34] such studies seem to make no impression upon the White House and Pentagon.

Public attitudes toward casualties are malleable, not rigid. Saddam Hussein's repeated miscalculations during the Gulf crisis stemmed in large measure from his twin convictions that Americans could not stand the sight of their own blood and that he was in a position to spill enough of it to collapse US domestic political support for war against Iraq.

Twentieth-century America has been prepared to expend the lives of over half a million of its sons to defeat totalitarian aggression in Europe and East Asia. Only during the Vietnam War did public support crack—and even then only after the shock of the Tet offensive, four years of apparent stalemate on the battlefield, and manifest official duplicity in Washington. Indeed, in retrospect it is amazing that public support remained

---

[34] See, for example, the following studies performed by RAND of Santa Monica, California: Mark Lorrell and Charles Kelley Jr., Casualties, Public Opinion, and Presidential Policy during the Vietnam War, March 1985; Benjamin C. Schwarz, Casualties, Public Opinion, and U.S. Military Intervention: Implications for U.S. Regional Deterrence Strategies, 1994; and Eric V. Larson, Casualties and Consensus: The Historical Role of Casualties in Domestic Support for U.S. Military Operations, 1996.

as strong as long as it did, given the war's geographic remoteness and the predominantly abstract quality of declared US war aims. Even after the cold war ended, President Bush mobilized substantial public and congressional support for going to war on behalf of a country little known to Americans. Although American casualties were miraculously low (146 killed in action), both the public and Capitol Hill were prepared to accept a much higher butcher's bill.[35] The Pentagon planned Operation Desert Storm, and the president authorized it on the assumption that American war dead possibly would number in the thousands.[36]

Recent polling data marshaled by the Project on the Gap between Military and Civilian Society, conducted by the Triangle Institute for Security Studies, confirms not only that "the strong belief of civilian and military elites that the American public will not support casualties is not supported by the survey data," but also that the "mass public says that it will accept casualties" in a variety of such scenarios.[37] The data further reveals that civilian policy makers—even more so, senior military officers—are much more casualty intolerant than the average American citizen.[38] The data was based on a survey of forty-nine hundred Americans drawn from three groups: senior or rising military

---

[35] See John E. Mueller, *Policy and Opinion in the Gulf War* (Chicago: University of Chicago Press, 1994), 45, 124, 306–7.

[36] Erdmann, 375–76.

[37] *Digest of Findings and Studies Presented to the Conference on the Military and Civilian Society*, Cantigny Conference Center, 1st Division Museum, 28–29 October 1999, 5; on-line, Internet, 12 November 1999, available from http://www.unc.edu/depts/tiss/CIVMIL.htm.

[38] Peter D. Feaver and Christopher Gelpi, "How Many Deaths Are Acceptable? A Surprising Answer," Washington Post, 7 November 1999.

officers, influential civilians, and the general public. Among the questions asked were, How many American military deaths would be acceptable to (1) stabilize a democratic government in the Congo, (2) prevent Iraq from obtaining weapons of mass destruction, and (3) defend Taiwan against an invasion by China? For the military elite, civilian elite, and the general public, the number of acceptable US military dead were, respectively, as follows: 284, 484, and 6,861 (Congo); 6,016, 19,045, and 29,853 (Iraq); and 17,425, 17,554, and 20,172 (Taiwan).[39]

Why do these elites appear to be more casualty sensitive than the people they serve? Is it because the assumption of the public's intolerance of casualties excuses presidents and generals from taking the kind of battlefield risks that might invite casualties? Because casualty avoidance offers an alibi for mission frustration and even failure? Because casualty phobia reinforces the argument against using force as a tool of coercive diplomacy? The authors of the Triangle Institute's poll speculate that senior military officers may lack confidence in the reliability of civilian leaders to stay the course of intervention if casualties mount. They also suspect that "casualty aversion may be an aspect of a growing zero-defect mentality among senior officers, in which casualties are not only deaths—they are an immediate indication that an operation is a failure." Obviously, "civilian leaders must share culpability" for any rise in a zero-defect mentality.[40]

---

[39] Ibid.
[40] Ibid.

Strategic Consequences of the Elite's Casualty Phobia

Because force-protection fetishism unnecessarily degrades military effectiveness, it emboldens enemies and poorly serves a great power that dozens of other states and hundreds of millions of people around the world look to for leadership and security. The Albanian Kosovars, to be sure, were victimized by Serbian thugs, but they were no less victimized, albeit indirectly, by the casualty phobia of US elites.

Force-protection fetishism encourages military half-measures directed against symptoms rather than sources of international political instability. This was as true of the Gulf War as it was of Allied Force. In both cases, the national leadership was not prepared to run the political and military risks necessary to achieve a strategically conclusive victory. Caution may well have been justified, but the chief consequence in the Gulf and the Balkans was the survival of two rogue regimes, one of them bent on massive revenge.

Anxiety over getting involved in a long and costly Arab conflict caused the Bush administration to end the war prematurely and with little thought of the politics of war termination. While the Iraqi army was in full retreat, the administration declared a unilateral cease-fire in the absence of any Baghdad request for terms and then sent Gen Norman Schwarzkopf—without political instructions—to Safwan, in enemy territory, to negotiate cease-fire terms with a bunch of Saddam Hussein's military flunkies. (Did it occur to no one that the Iraqis should have been summoned to appear at Schwarzkopf's headquarters and told that a cease-fire required, among other things, an acknowledgement of defeat by Saddam himself?) The administration failed to take advantage of potentially decisive leverage in forcing Saddam's ouster, and it permitted the Iraqis to continue flying their attack helicopters, which they promptly used to crush the subsequent Shia rebellion in southern Iraq.[41]

The Gulf War has been touted as a model display of the Weinberger-Powell Doctrine in action. And so it was in many respects. After all, at the time Powell himself was CJCS, and he was given great latitude in designing and implementing Desert Storm. For the Gulf War, the doctrine made sense. Any president contemplating a major war against an apparently formidable enemy would be foolish indeed to launch such a war over trivial interests without public and congressional support and without a convincing diplomatic exhaustion of nonwar alternatives. At the same time, however, the rush to declare military victory and vacate the premises underscored the Vietnam Syndrome's continued affliction of the White House and Pentagon—an affliction that precluded a strategically conclusive success. Thus, the war against Iraq never quite ended; it has continued for nine years (and counting) in the form of repeated US packages of punitive air and missile strikes and the ongoing, costly occupation of Iraqi airspace to keep Saddam Hussein "in his box."

Indeed, there might not have been any US involvement or war at all had the decision been Powell's to make. He would have permitted Iraqi aggression to stand. Powell feared a possible US

---

[41] Administration officials hoped that the coalition's military victory, which at the end of the war appeared more decisive than it actually was, would prompt a coup against Saddam. At the same time, the Shia and Kurdish rebellions portended Iraq's possible disintegration— something the White House most assuredly did not want. What the administration wanted was an intact Iraq without Saddam.

military embarrassment in the Gulf and lacked confidence that the American people and their elected representatives could be trusted to support whatever military action it took to expel Iraqi forces from Kuwait. Accordingly, he waged a subtle bureaucratic campaign against going to war. During the deployment phase of the crisis, he pushed for sanctions as an alternative to war and encouraged the submission of war plans that he believed, or at least hoped, would deter his civilian superiors from deciding for war.[42] Two months after Iraq invaded Kuwait, Powell told Sir Patrick Hine, Britain's air chief marshal, that the risks of war, including a high death toll, possible degeneration into attrition, and losing the peace, were simply too great.[43] Powell, of course, went on to oppose any US military intervention in the former Yugoslavia.

The consequences of elite groups' fear of casualties in the former Yugoslavia (read fear of a Balkan Vietnam) were evident

---

[42] The plans included Schwarzkopf's initial unimaginative, Army-developed ground-war plan and, later, a second plan calling for doubling the size of the US deployment from a defensive to an offensive force. Brent Scowcroft, national security advisor, suspected the plans were deliberately crafted to discourage war: "The initial plan for retaking Kuwait, briefed to President Bush in October, had not seemed designed by anyone eager to undertake the task. Similarly, the force requirements for a successful offense given to him at the end of October were so large that one could speculate that they were set forth by a command [US Central Command] hoping their size would change his [Bush's] mind about pursuing a military option." George Bush and Brent Scowcroft, A World Transformed (New York: Alfred A. Knopf, 1998), 431.

[43] For the best informed account of Powell's behind-the-scenes campaign to derail the Bush administration's drive toward war in the Gulf, see Michael R. Gordon and Bernard E. Trainor, The Generals' War: The Inside Story of the Conflict in the Gulf (Boston: Little, Brown and Company, 1995), 123–58.

years before the launching of Allied Force. James Gow, who has written the best diplomatic history of the "Yugoslav War of Dissolution," concludes that "if there was an overall policy failure, its central feature was the absence of armed force as a bottom line. The reason for that absence was a lack of 'political will' to act forcefully in a transitional situation that appeared to be . . . laced with risk." And to what was that lack of will attributable? To the fear of Western politicians that what lay waiting for them in the Balkans was "another Northern Ireland, Dien Bien Phu, or broader Vietnam," and "particularly critical in this respect was the shadow of Vietnam hanging over US political and military leaders."[44]

To put it another way, the United States and its principal European allies failed repeatedly to make credible threats of force against Serbian aggressors because in fact they were clearly unwilling to actually use force in a convincing manner. Accordingly, Milosevic called the West's bluff repeatedly and successfully during the war in Bosnia and later rejected NATO's ultimatum on Kosovo. NATO's record of political division and military faintheartedness over events in the former Yugoslavia persisted into Allied Force in both the White House's public renunciation of a ground-force option and the initially tepid air "campaign" against Serbia. Is it any wonder that Milosevic refused to fold early (as Secretary of State Madeleine Albright and some of the administration officials expected)[45] and

---

[44] James Gow, *Triumph of the Lack of Will: International Diplomacy and the Yugoslav War* (New York: Columbia University Press, 1997), 306.

[45] See John F. Harris, "Reassuring Rhetoric, Reality in Conflict," Washington Post, 8 April 1999.

successfully held out for terms significantly more favorable to Belgrade than those NATO insisted upon at Rambouillet?[46]

If force-protection fetishism saved Milosevic and spared the Serbian army (which departed Kosovo virtually intact and saluting victory), it has also distinguished the US component on the United Nations peacekeeping force established in Kosovo after the war. In Bosnia, unlike other national contingents, most of the US troops were based at a 775-acre, heavily fortified but exceptionally comfortable site from which they were permitted to venture outside only with body armor and Kevlar helmets— and even then only in helicopters or convoys of armored vehicles. These force-protection measures hindered the troops' ability to perform peacekeeping tasks. In contrast, the British, long experienced in imperial policing operations and unconstrained by a political or military leadership petrified at the prospect of taking casualties, were widely dispersed in their sector, with small groups billeted in apartments and houses in tense local neighborhoods. They patrolled on foot in small numbers without armored vests or helmets, which put them in much closer touch with local residents and events. The US obsession with zero casualties became the butt of jokes by officers from European peacekeeping contingents.[47]

---

[46] Among the demands contained in the NATO ultimatum issued to Serbia at Rambouillet before the war was restoration of Kosovo's autonomy. Following this, three years later, was a referendum in Kosovo to determine its future and a provision granting NATO forces unrestricted passage and unimpeded access throughout all of Serbia— not just Kosovo. These provisions were subsequently dropped as conditions of war termination.

[47] See R. Jeffrey Smith, "A GI's Home Is His Fortress," Washington Post, 5 October 1999.

Clausewitz reminded his readers that war is "a serious means to a serious end."[48] Does elevation of force protection to first place among all other operational objectives convey a seriousness of means? Does it not instead signal to adversary and ally alike the presence of a frail will? Does it not encourage enemies to adopt the simple strategy of filling as many American body bags as possible? And what does it matter that the average American is more casualty tolerant than the senior US political and military leadership? If that leadership is more concerned about the safety of its military means than a decisive attainment of its political ends, has not the United States become, in the words of Richard Nixon, "a pitiful, helpless giant?"

Remedies for Force-Protection Fetishism?

No obvious cure exists for the affliction of casualty phobia. Hopefully, the elites themselves will come to recognize that the public's tolerance for casualties is much more contingent than pessimists believe or want to believe, and that the political leadership can greatly influence public attitudes on casualties in a given situation. Given the strength of the elite's conviction that the people they serve have little stomach for war under almost any circumstances, however, it would probably take an actual demonstration of casualty tolerance to change minds. But this hardly means seeking another war just to prove a point. Moreover, the United States is fast running out of enemies capable of inflicting significant casualties on deployed US military forces.

A more promising approach to the strategic problem posed by force-protection fetishism would be greater US cultivation of

---

[48] Clausewitz, 86.

and reliance on local surrogates to assume the risks of ground combat. The Nixon Doctrine makes as much sense now as it ever did, and we should not forget the Reagan Doctrine's success in Afghanistan. Of course, surrogate forces are only occasionally available and have their own political agendas. But when they are willing and (with training and assistance) able to fight a common enemy, they limit America's potential military liabilities in circumstances in which domestic political tolerance of US casualties is—or is believed to be—severely limited. Perhaps the Clinton administration's greatest squandered opportunity in the Balkans was its refusal to arm and train the victims of Serbian aggression. Arming the Bosnian Muslims and later the Kosovo Liberation Army, as well as supporting both with US airpower when necessary, would have been power balancing, pure and simple. But it would have provided an earlier and more effective check on Serbian behavior in Bosnia and Kosovo than the actual policy of hiding behind an ineffective international arms embargo of all of the former Yugoslavia and showering Belgrade with incredible threats of force.

To be sure, backing surrogates entails taking sides. But the history of international politics shows that the most effective means of thwarting bids for hegemony is to create situations of countervailing strength. When the United States can do so by developing local surrogates instead of committing its own forces, it should do so unless there is some compelling strategic or political reason not to. And yes, there is always the risk of surrogate failure, confronting the United States with the choice of either walking away altogether or committing its own forces. This is precisely what happened in Vietnam, where the United States picked a politically and militarily incompetent client threatened by a skilled and determined adversary. Indeed, once the United States took over the war, the South Vietnamese army had little incentive to fight. Circumstances in the former Yugoslavia, however, were quite the opposite—yet the Vietnam War blinded policy makers.

A final observation on force-protection fetishism: to the extent that casualty phobia persists and to the extent that it continues to promote—as it did in the war against Serbia—reliance on airpower to the exclusion of ground-combat forces, then we need to take a new look at the present proportional allocation of resources to US ground and air forces. If in combat the United States is going to be a one-armed superpower, then that arm should be as strong as possible.

Politics, Death, and Morality in US Foreign Policy

by Karl P. Mueller

Also in the summer of 2000, the Aerospace Power Journal published this article by Karl Mueller, who is nowadays an associate director at the Rand Corporation. The Journal wrote:

> In this companion piece to Dr. Record's article on "Force-Protection Fetishism," Dr. Mueller provides a balanced perspective on casualty aversion and its potential implications in military operations and on national security policy. He argues that aversion has become "cultish" due largely to technological changes in warfare that make it more feasible and, therefore, a moral imperative to conduct less brutish combat. Yet, he points out that moral obligation may just as well dictate dying for the right cause and that such morality, rather than politically expedient doctrines, should drive our policy.

AMERICAN NATIONAL LEADERS, both military and civilian, appear to be held in thrall by a cult of casualty avoidance, as Jeffrey Record compellingly argues in slightly different words in his article "Force-Protection Fetishism" (this issue). To call it a cult is not mere hyperbole. Many statesmen and generals believe, with absolute and unquestioning conviction, that the United States can no longer use force successfully unless American military casualties are virtually nil, even though there is little evidence to support this belief and in spite of its pernicious effects on US foreign and defense policy.[49]

The belief that the United States will avoid risking the lives of its troops, and will capitulate if they are killed in quantity, encourages America's enemies by offering an apparent means to defeat the numerically and technologically superior superpower. It also divides the United States from allies who do not share this belief about themselves. So buying into the myth is an act of pessimism—even of defeatism—although, of course, statesmen have often held erroneously pessimistic beliefs before. What is more surprising is that the casualty-avoidance cult is so powerful among military leaders when, as Record notes, it threatens the very existence of the US Army (and arguably the Marine Corps as well) as we know it. It also holds the potential to transform the combat arms of the US Air Force into mere deliverers of standoff munitions and operators of uninhabited aircraft. Such a transition might conceivably make military sense, but one certainly would not expect it to appeal to traditional fighter or bomber generals.

Of course, like most myths, the belief in American casualty intolerance is constructed around a kernel of truth. US public

---

[49] On the reality of US casualty intolerance, see, in addition to the sources cited by Record, Troy E. DeVine, "The Influence of America's Casualty Sensitivity on Military Strategy and Doctrine" (master's thesis, School of Advanced Airpower Studies, June 1997); and John Mueller, "Public Opinion as a Constraint on U.S. Foreign Policy: Assessing the Perceived Value of U.S. and Foreign Lives" (paper presented at the International Studies Association National Convention, Los Angeles, Calif., 14 March 2000). On the historically more common military tendency towards cultish beliefs in the omnipotence of the offense, see Maj John R. Carter, *Airpower and the Cult of the Offensive* (Maxwell AFB, Ala.: Air University Press, 1998).

support for wars that seem inordinately costly relative to their objectives—or that appear to offer little prospect of success— has indeed disintegrated as body counts have risen, most visibly in Korea, Vietnam, Lebanon, and Somalia— although this pattern is neither unique to the United States nor a product of the television age, as is often suggested.[50] However, historical experience offers no reason to believe that the American public will fail to support costly wars in which the lives of US troops are not apparently being wasted. Moreover, public-opinion evidence indicates that Americans have been largely indifferent to loss of life among allied forces, enemy troops, and civilian populations although, again, US leaders often believe the opposite to be true.

Behind the Cult

Why, then, do the myths of casualty and collateral-damage intolerance hold such sway? In fact, there are many reasons for the cult. In part, it grows out of paying too much attention to a small number of high-profile cases without placing them in proper context. And, in part, it has to do with many politicians, military leaders, and journalists being undereducated in history and social science. But it also reflects larger historical and technological trends: the increasing potential cleanliness of warfare and the West's slow, on-going shift away from barbarism.

---

[50] The relationship between the decline in US public support for the televised Vietnam War and the accumulation of casualties in the conflict was roughly the same as occurred in Korea, during the age of radio and newsreels. See John E. Mueller, *War, Presidents, and Public Opinion* (New York: Wiley, 1973).

Although the idea that warfare is becoming less gruesome may seem counterintuitive at first glance, it is generally true. During the last two hundred years, both conventional land and naval combat have grown progressively (though not always steadily) less horrible for their participants in the developed world, thanks to factors such as improved medical care and casualty evacuation, mechanization, and refinements in some classes of weapons. Air warfare, too, has become a far less bloody activity over its 90 years of development. In short, the lives of soldiers have, on the whole, become less nasty, brutish, and short since the beginning of the industrial revolution, as have the peacetime lives of civilians. Warfare has also tended to become less brutal for noncombatants, except of course when they are deliberately targeted; particularly in recent years, the ability of armed forces to minimize harm to civilians when at-tacking their enemies has improved dramatically as a result of the revolution in precision-guided weapons. Of course, none of this means that a particular war will be less horrible than those that preceded it—only that it can be.

Along with this increasing potential for the human costs of warfare to decline has come a normative belief that they should do so and that war, widely considered a morally uplifting entertainment as recently as a century ago, is something that ought in general to be avoided—or at least controlled.[51] The more casualties can and should be avoided, the more justification they require and the more unacceptable the profligate waste of soldiers' lives becomes.

---

[51] See John E. Mueller, *Retreat from Doomsday: The Obsolescence of Major War* (New York: Basic Books, 1989).

Thus, in some ways, a faulty or exaggerated belief in total casualty intolerance can be seen as something hopeful—as giving Americans credit for even greater aversion to death and killing than they actually deserve. However, it has a far less laudable side as well, representing the dominance of political expediency over morality, assuming moral cowardice on the part of the American people, and shifting blame onto the public for the military and political failures of statesmen and generals.

Making a Virtue of Timidity

Jeffrey Record attributes many of the failures of Operation Allied Force—most notably the failure to halt the expulsion of the Albanian Kosovars—to the unwillingness of the United States and the North Atlantic Treaty Organization (NATO) to place the lives of ground troops at risk, and to the air campaign's priority on minimizing alliance losses by operating at medium and high altitudes. These are reasonable charges although it is not certain that a less cautious air campaign would have achieved better political results, even if it had been more effective at destroying Serbian ground forces. Nor can we yet be sure that the "no ground forces" pledge actually lengthened the war, although it may well have—Slobodan Milosevic probably would have doubted NATO's will to invade Serbia until Anglo-American intentions to do so were made clear late in the war, regardless of the ill-advised rhetoric coming from the White House and Brussels in the early weeks of the conflict. And an early combined-arms attack into Kosovo might have produced a far greater bloodbath for the Kosovars than actually occurred. Nevertheless, a pervasive fear of casualties, along with efforts to avoid causing civilian deaths, certainly dominated both the air campaign and Milosevic's strategy to make NATO call off the war.

Next door to Serbia, in Bosnia, the effects of the force-protection mania are also visible in a way that is less dramatic but at least as disturbing. As Record describes, if American troops often appear afraid to emerge from their compound except in heavily armed, multivehicle convoys in spite of Bosnia's low-threat environment, they can contribute little to real peacekeeping. The US military stands poised to cross the line from being the world's slightly uneasy sheriff to its downright nervous Barney Fife.

However, in both the Serbian and Bosnian cases, among others, it may not be the effects of casualty-averse US policies that are the most troubling, but their motivations. In one briefing and press conference after another, both military and civilian leaders explain their efforts to protect the lives of American troops in terms of the political unpopularity of suffering casualties, painting a picture of an American public that is too craven to make

noble sacrifices on its own and too ignorant to grasp leaders' explanations of why it should. Similarly, NATO's Herculean efforts to avoid causing collateral damage during Operations Deliberate Force and Allied Force were usually justified on the grounds that they were required in order to keep the international media and the allied powers happy. Among other effects, emphasizing the political rather than the moral imperatives to avoid killing noncombatants threatens to create a litigious mind-set among air campaign planners that assumes that if a target is legal to attack, it must be worth attacking.

Does the American public really demand that the lives of US troops and those of civilians not be wasted? Will the press have a field day if civilians are killed by US bombing? At the most fundamental level, it should not matter. We certainly ought to protect our forces and protect noncombatants, insofar as we can, regardless of popular opinion—not be-cause doing so is politically prudent but be-cause it is morally right.

Conversely, however, there are objectives that are worth dying—and killing—in order to achieve; in such cases, it is morally wrong not to risk or take lives when necessary. To shy away from casualties under these circumstances strikes at the very heart of American soldiers' solemn oath to defend their country from all enemies. Moreover, to blame such a lack of national courage on the imaginary squeamishness of the electorate calls into question the philosophical foundation of the Republic itself.

Reassessing the Morality of War

Record rightly savages the Weinberger-Powell Doctrine over its prescriptions to use military force only when the most vital national interests are at stake and only when public and legislative opinion favor the use of force. As he argues, these criteria would have supported the disastrous Anglo-French appeasement of Hitler at Munich in 1938, and they probably would have suggested that US intervention in Vietnam was a good idea.[52]

(Moreover, although Weinberger himself disagrees, a good case can be made that all of his doctrine's criteria were eventually

---

[52] At least early in the conflict. After the fall of Sukarno and the Indonesian communists in 1964, the argument that keeping South Vietnam noncommunist was vital to US national interests became less tenable.

75

fulfilled during Operation Allied Force.)[53] One could add that if the Weinberger Doctrine had held sway in the 1770s, the American Revolution— initially supported by only a third or so of the colonists—would never have been under-taken. Endorsing the use of overwhelming force to protect vital interests while prohibiting the use of limited force for more modest ends does indeed tie the hands of statesmen both unnecessarily and inappropriately, subordinating pursuit of the national interest to protection of the government's popularity.

The last of Weinberger's six criteria also merits reexamination: the widely accepted rule that commitment of US forces to combat should be a policy of last resort. Although the "last resort" mantra has a certain absolutist appeal, it is in fact a fatally flawed principle. If the reason for making force a last resort is simply to avoid suffering casualties unless there is no alternative, then American states-men should consider using military force in many situations in which it can be effectively employed without risk of harm to US forces, a potentially common circumstance in the post-cold-war world of weak enemies and powerful standoff weapons. Moreover, putting US forces in harm's way is almost never truly a last resort—there are always alternatives for the world's only superpower. The fact that for 50 years the United States has opted to suffer casualties in a number of conventional conflicts that could easily have been settled by using nuclear weapons is but one clear indication that we do not actually believe that spilling American blood must be avoided at all costs short of surrender.

---

[53] See Caspar W. Weinberger, "The Use of Force—The Six Criteria Revisited," speech at the Air Force Association National Convention, Washington, D.C., 14 September 1999; on-line, Internet, 14 March 2000, available from http://www.aef.org/ wein999.html.

On the other hand, if the last-resort rule is based on the moral premise that military force is too destructive to employ unless all else has failed, it provides poor guidance in cases in which military force has the potential to inflict less harm than alternative policies. For example, in some circumstances, as was true in the 1990–91 confrontation with Iraq over Kuwait, using force sooner rather than later can be less costly than trying everything else first. Moreover, it is important to recognize that in this era of discriminate weapons, the use of force can be far less destructive than employing some other, supposedly milder, instruments of power—most notably wide-spectrum economic sanctions. This is strikingly illustrated by Western policy towards Iraq in the 1990s, when United Nations trade restrictions indirectly led to the deaths of hundreds of thousands of Iraqi civilians, in the wake of a far more effective air war that killed only thousands of them.[54] As airpower continues to develop its precision-targeting and -attack capabilities, and as nonlethal weapons enter the military inventory, the traditional association of military force with maximum destruction will become increasingly outdated, and the last-resort principle will eventually have to be abandoned.

Making Moral Strategy

If the American public is conditionally tolerant of casualties and consistently indifferent to collateral damage, and if the central principles of the Weinberger Doctrine are little more than a list of excuses for avoiding political risk, what should guide US decisions about when and how to use military force? Inconveniently for national decision makers, the answer is that

---

[54] See John Mueller and Karl Mueller, "Sanctions of Mass Destruction," Foreign Affairs, May/June 1999, 43–53.

these choices call not for simple rules of thumb but for actual wisdom. Deciding which causes are worth risking American lives to pursue and what amount of risk is appropriate ultimately requires a moral, not simply a political, compass.

This is not to say that public opinion is irrelevant—in a sound democracy it cannot be. However, national leaders are obligated to lead. When they do so, they generally find that the populace is quite tolerant of their foreign-policy decisions. In fact, the American people will even support military actions that are ill advised, requiring statesmen and generals to provide their own restraints on adventurism, although these ought to be more sophisticated and well founded than those embodied in the cult of the defensive or the Weinberger-Powell Doctrine.

The best defense against losing public support for military actions once casualties begin to occur is popular conviction of their compelling moral value. To a considerable extent, this can be shaped by effective leaders, although history also teaches that the American people are not amoral dupes who will credulously accept anything they are told. Expensive wars are often acceptable, while apparently pointless or disproportionately ex-pensive wars are not. In the end, however, the assumption that the public will not support doing that which is right is simply unacceptable as a basis for national policy. If it were consistently true, the United States would not deserve the protection of those who have pledged their lives to defend it.

Casualty Aversion

Implications for Policy Makers and Senior Military Officers

Maj. Charles K. Hyde, USAF

Rounding out the "aversion" pieces in the summer of 2000, the Aerospace Power Journal published this article by Charles Hyde which emphasized the false underpinnings of the casualty phobia Jeffrey Record pinned on the "elites." Hyde dives more deeply into data alluded to in earlier pieces. Today he is a brigadier general and wing commander.

The Journal introduced his piece this way:

> In this article, both a survey of casualty-aversion studies and an analysis of the American casualty-awareness syndrome, Major Hyde argues for a clear recognition of what drives casualty consciousness on the part of political and military decision makers and the civilian populace at large. Involving more than reaction to alarming numbers or pictures, this consciousness is part of a calculation of perceived benefits as portrayed in our democratic process. More importantly, the author addresses the negative implication that unwarranted casualty aversion potentially has on operational planning and execution. In essence, casualty aversion leads to casualty displacement because those who should take on the casualty burden fundamental to their mission and professional ethos shift that obligation to others who have inherited a more vulnerable situation.

THE EVENTS OF the last one hundred years have witnessed dramatic changes in American foreign policy and, in particular, the use of force in support of national objectives. From a sleeping giant with overt isolationist tendencies prior to World War II, the United States has evolved at the beginning of the twenty-first century into the world's only superpower. The transition from a body politic wedded to the charge of George Washington's farewell address that we should avoid "entangling alliances" to a recognized superpower with global interests and responsibilities has been marked by the commitment of the United States to stand up for its values and principles with military might. This might, in combination with other elements of national power, defeated Nazism and Japanese hegemony in World War II and hastened the end of the cold war, which saw the collapse of Soviet-dominated communism and global bipolar confrontation.

The end of the cold war, however, unleashed an uncertain world that has not developed into a new world order or seen the end of conflicts. Challenges to the interests of the United States and free people around the world remain, and the United States is currently positioned as the only nation with the global capabilities and power to provide leadership for an uncertain future. As stated in A National Security Strategy for a New Century, "Our nation's challenge—and our responsibility—is to sustain that role by harnessing the forces of global integration for the benefit of our own people and people around the world."[55] In order to meet these challenges and remain the

---

[55] Executive Office of the President, *A National Security Strategy for a New Century* (Washington, D.C.: The White House, 1998), iii.

"world's most powerful force for peace, prosperity and the universal values of democracy and freedom" that the president's strategy champions,[56] the United States has to show leadership in an anarchical world by acting like a great power.

Since the fall of the Berlin Wall and the demise of global communism, many countries have challenged the ability of the United States to maintain its position as world leader. Conventional wisdom has it that the United States is unwilling to commit the military power required to influence events, settle disputes, and act as the force for democracy, peace, and economic freedom that our national strategy promulgates. The perception among our enemies and allies alike is that the American public is unwilling to commit to any military operation in which one can expect even a minimal number of casualties. Furthermore, they believe that once an enemy engages the United States, it can force the latter to withdraw from its commitments when American casualties mount. Because of our casualty aversion, in the eyes of the world, we are becoming "a sawdust superpower."[57]

In light of the changing environment in which military and security policy is conducted, the Triangle Institute for Strategic Studies (TISS) recently conducted a study on civil-military relations. As part of that study, several scholars studied casualty aversion and concluded that the American public is far more tolerant of potential casualties than are policy makers or senior military officers. In a Washington Post article, two of the

---

[56] Ibid.
[57] Mark J. Conversino, "Sawdust Superpower: Perceptions of U.S. Casualty Tolerance in the Post–Gulf War Era," Strategic Review, Winter 1997, 22.

principal TISS researchers stated that the common belief that the American public demands "a casualty-free victory as the price of supporting any military intervention abroad" is a myth.[58]

If true, the TISS findings have significant implications. Does a casualty-aversion syndrome exist? If so, what are the implications for policy makers and senior military commanders? In the broadest sense, these are the issues examined in this article. TISS data is consistent with research that sheds light on the casualty-aversion issue. By examining the existing body of research, this article argues that policy makers and senior military leaders have misinterpreted the public's casualty tolerance and that their incorrect view of casualty aversion adversely affects national security and military operations.

Casualties and Public Opinion

Do our civilian and military leaders have a sound case for believing that public opinion is linked to the number of casualties suffered in a military operation? Several RAND studies have examined this issue by consolidating available research and drawing conclusions based on the data. The first significant report, published in 1985, used Korea and Vietnam as case studies.[59] The overall decline of public support over time in Korea and Vietnam shows that public support in both wars "behaved in a remarkably similar manner: Every time U.S.

---

[58] Peter D. Feaver and Christopher Gelpi, "A Look at Casualty Aversion: How Many Deaths Are Acceptable? A Surprising Answer," Washington Post, 7 November 1999, B3.
[59] Mark Lorell and Charles Kelley Jr., with Deborah Hensler, Casualties, Public Opinion, and Presidential Policy during the Vietnam War, R-3060-AF (Santa Monica, Calif.: RAND, March 1985), 1–92.

casualties went up by a factor of ten, support in both wars decreased by approximately 15 percent."[60] Likewise, comparing public support for Vietnam with the cumulative costs of the war leads to the conclusion one would hope for in a civilized society: "The most significant costs to the American people were the number of American boys killed and wounded in Vietnam."[61] Finally, analyzing monthly casualty rates indicates "a strong negative correlation (−.68) was shown to exist between monthly casualty rates and president Truman's popularity in the Korean War."[62] In a companion finding, President Lyndon Johnson's popularity was negatively correlated to the monthly number of Americans killed in action and the number of bombing sorties over Vietnam.[63]

The research documented in the 1985 RAND study concluded that the public was sensitive to casualties and gradually withdrew its support of military operations in Korea and Vietnam, based on the cumulative number of causalities. The study made a significant contextual point of the limited-war environment in which these conflicts took place. Analysis of the data by RAND researchers led to the conclusion that "the public tends to be unwilling to tolerate anything more than minimal costs in limited war situations."[64] From this perspective, it is easy to discern the roots of a casualty-aversion syndrome. Were this the only research, it would be difficult to refute the common belief among our policy makers, senior military leaders, allies, and enemies that casualty aversion is the

---

[60] Ibid., 21.
[61] Ibid.
[62] Ibid., 23.
[63] Ibid.
[64] Ibid., vii.

Achilles' heel of the United States. The study, however, did not address several key variables: the reasons underlying the support for relatively high casualties for a significant length of time, the impact of public disapproval on alternative courses of action, and the impact of other variables that could have influenced public opinion.

Another RAND study by Benjamin Schwarz in 1994 dealt with the question of alternative courses of action that the public may have supported in the Korean, Vietnam, and Gulf Wars.[65] This report analyzed the earlier study's conclusion that the American public is casualty-averse and postulated that the perceived casualty aversion affected regional deterrence strategies. If adversaries believe they can defeat America or force it to withdraw from a military intervention by imposing casualties on US forces, "then they are unlikely to be deterred by U.S. threats to intervene."[66] This fear emerged prior to the Gulf War, when Saddam Hussein remained undeterred and boasted to the US ambassador to Iraq on 25 July 1990 "about Iraq's readiness to fight any foe over honor, 'regardless of the cost,' while America, unable to stomach '10,000 dead in one battle' was incapable of pursuing a major war to a successful conclusion."[67] Saddam was wrong, but his perception of American casualty aversion hurt our ability to deter Iraqi aggression.

Schwarz contends that the public became "disillusioned" with America's participation in Korea and Vietnam and regretted the decision to intervene but actually rejected withdrawal in favor

---

[65] Benjamin C. Schwarz, Casualties, Public Opinion, & U.S. Military Intervention, MR-431-A/AF (Santa Monica, Calif.: RAND, 1994), 1–27.
[66] Ibid., 4.
[67] Conversino, 17.

of escalation of the conflicts. He states that "there was, however, very little movement in the percentage of Americans polled who wished the United States to withdraw from the conflict. In fact, a growing number of Americans favored escalation of the conflicts to bring them to a quick—and victorious—end."[68] Backing up this assertion was selective polling data showing that a majority of Americans supported escalation over withdrawal in Korea and Vietnam and preferred escalation of US war aims in the Gulf, including the removal of Saddam from power. Rather than fitting the American casualty-aversion perception, this data implies the opposite.

In 1996 Eric Larson completed a comprehensive RAND study that attempted to explain the disparity among research studies conducted up to that year.[69] He examined the results of public-opinion polls taken from World War II through the military intervention in Somalia, seeking to determine if other variables accounted for the differences in support documented in US military interventions. The conventional wisdom, alluded to earlier, is that the American public has changed since World War II and will no longer accept interventions that produce casualties. A perceived corollary is that Americans will demand immediate withdrawal when casualties mount during operations. Larson investigated these issues by developing a model explaining public support for military interventions in terms of a broader context.

---

[68] Ibid., ix.

[69] Eric V. Larson, *Casualties and Consensus: The Historical Role of Casualties in Domestic Support for U.S. Military Operations*, MR-726-RC (Santa Monica, Calif.: RAND, 1996), 1–126.

Larson's model weighs the dynamics of public support within a simple calculation of ends and means. In this model, the public bases support for an intervention on a rational consideration of five factors:

- Perceived benefits of the intervention.

- Prospects for success.

- Prospective and actual costs.

- Changing expectations.

- Leadership and cueing from political leaders.[70]

This simple calculus captures the many variables that interact to produce public support. Using this approach means that "support can be thought of as a constant rebalancing of the benefits and prospects for success against the likely and actual costs—and a determination of whether the outcome is judged worth the costs."[71]

This model of ends and means is embedded within the concept of a "democratic conversation." The argument, supported by research, states that "political leaders lead the democratic conversation, the political discourse . . . is observed and reported by the media, [and] as members of the public are exposed to these messages, attitudes change in a predictable fashion."[72] This does not imply that society is a pawn in the

---

[70] Ibid., 10–12; and Eric V. Larson, "Ends and Means in the Democratic Conversation: Understanding the Role of Casualties in Support of U.S. Military Operations" (PhD diss., RAND Graduate School, 1996), 320.
[71] Larson, Casualties and Consensus, 12.
[72] Larson, "Ends and Means," 267.

hands of wily politicians but that the public takes cues from credible political leaders who have a similar worldview or political ideology. "In short, individuals ultimately choose which arguments are most credible but use a shortcut that reduces their information-gathering costs."[73] The implication is that public casualty aversion does not drive support for military interventions. The public is able to rationally discern the merits of each individual case and make an informed determination of support, based on expectations, benefits, prospects, and costs.

Using this conceptual framework, Larson determined that the American public has not become more casualty-averse since World War II. Indeed, Americans have always had a high regard for human life, but they balance that regard within a continuous cost-benefit analysis which ultimately determines support. It is only logical that increasing costs in terms of casualties will result in a decline in public support unless an increase in the benefits or prospects for success offsets that cost. This explains the differences in support for various interventions since World War II and also explains the general decrease in support over time as casualties mount in a particular operation. As the RAND study states,

Less well understood, however, is the fact that the importance of casualties to support has varied greatly across operations; when important interests and principles have been at stake, the public has been willing to tolerate rather high casualties. In short, when we take into account the importance of the perceived benefits, the evidence of a recent decline in the

---

[73] Larson, Casualties and Consensus, 75.

willingness of the public to tolerate casualties appears rather thin.[74]

One sees World War II as a departure point with regard to casualty aversion because of the extremely high levels of support despite enormous losses (table 1).

TABLE 1	
US PERSONNEL KILLED IN ACTION (KIA)	
WORLD WAR II	291,557
KOREA	33,651
VIETNAM	47,364
GRENADA	16
PANAMA	24
[FIRST GULF WAR]	293

Source: Figures taken from Karl W. Eikenberry, "Take No Casualties," Parameters 26, no. 2 (Summer 1996): 113.

In the light of the casualty figures, World War II appears to be an exception—in some way different from the limited conflicts of the cold war and recent interventions characterized by a decline in support as costs increased. In fact, one can attribute the nearly consistent public support despite dramatically rising casualties in 1944 and 1945 to the increasing prospects for victory, based on battlefield accomplishments in Europe and the Pacific, anticipated benefits of unconditional surrender, and near-unanimous political support from both parties. "In short, as the costs increased, these costs were compensated by increasing war aims and prospects for success."[75]

---

[74] Ibid., 49.
[75] Larson, "Ends and Means," 167.

Likewise, polling data from Korea and Vietnam supports the assertion that the public weighed the merits of each intervention, using a cost-benefit analysis. Both wars started with a significant level of support, based on the important US interest of "containing communist expansion," and both "contained the risk of a dramatic increase in costs if there were to be an expansion of the war to involve China or Russia."[76] In Korea, support increased as the prospects for success rose after Inchon, the potential benefit including a unified peninsula. Conversely, after the Chinese intervention, support declined, based on dimming prospects for gains beyond the status quo. As a stalemate developed, political opposition increased, and public support declined. The RAND study of 1996 noted that although casualty costs were important in declining support, "their influence cannot be untangled from these other factors."[77]

Support for the Vietnam conflict also mirrors the ends-and-means calculus reflected in the Korean War. Dwindling prospects for success as the war continued, a decrease in the perceived benefit of containing communism and improving relations with China, and the dramatic division among political leaders all led to decreasing support for the war. Casualties, although important, were not the sole determinant of public support, suggesting a potential problem with conventional wisdom which asserts that the American public will demand immediate withdrawal when casualties rise.

In both Korea and Vietnam, America continued the struggle long after support for the interventions had declined below 50

---

[76] Larson, Casualties and Consensus, 24.
[77] Ibid., 23.

percent. There was no consensus or immediate withdrawal or escalation to victory. What happened? In essence, the American public weighed the ends and means and supported a policy of negotiated settlement and orderly withdrawal. Larson points out that only a minority of the populace supported the extreme positions of immediate withdrawal or escalation, "while pluralities or majorities ('the Silent Majority') occupied a centrist position."[78]

If Korea and Vietnam fit within the framework of ends and means, as well as democratic conversation about support for military interventions, then Somalia becomes the chief evidence of those who proclaim that the public, swayed by Cable News Network (CNN), will cut and run at the first sign of blood. Analyzing the "CNN effect" is beyond the scope of this article, but detailed research indicates that rather than setting the agenda, CNN reports responded to the actions of the White House, Congress, and the State Department[79] in a manner consistent with democratic conversation.

Common perception has it that the death of 18 US soldiers in Somalia in October 1993 caused the public to demand immediate withdrawal from that country. This view misses the fact that support had already collapsed before the firefight in Mogadishu, with only 40 percent of the public supporting the operation.[80] Changing expectations caused by the shift in mission focus from popular humanitarian objectives to nation building and warlord hunting, combined with congressional "cues" against the operation (both houses of Congress passed

---

[78] Ibid., 65.
[79] Larson, "Ends and Means," 245–51.
[80] Ibid., 248.

nonbinding resolutions calling on the president to articulate his objectives and exit strategy in September 1993)[81] had already doomed the intervention. Larson states that

> Somalia represents another case in which the historical record suggests a more sensible and subtle response to increasing casualties and declining support: A plurality or majority has typically rejected both extreme options of escalation and immediate withdrawal and has remained unwilling to withdraw until a negotiated settlement and orderly withdrawal—including the return of U.S. servicemen—could be concluded.[82]

Thus, recent research supports the contention that the public does not demand bloodless interventions as the starting point for securing national interests and exercising world leadership, as articulated in our National Security Strategy. The public has consistently operated within the realm of an ends-and-means evaluation with significant cues from political leaders who frame the public debate.

The Casualty Myth

If the public is not casualty-averse, as the evidence suggests, the focus turns to the misinterpretation of this fact by our national security leadership. The TISS study provides strong evidence that policy makers and senior military leaders believe that the American public is casualty-averse and will not tolerate deaths except when vital interests are at stake. The study reached this conclusion by posing three plausible intervention scenarios (defending Taiwan against a Chinese invasion, preventing Iraq

---

[81] Ibid.
[82] Larson, Casualties and Consensus, 72.

from acquiring weapons of mass destruction, and stabilizing a democratic government in the Congo) to senior military officers, influential civilian leaders, and the general public and by asking them to consider how many American deaths would be acceptable to complete each mission (table 2).

TABLE 2			
NUMBER OF DEATHS ACCEPTABLE			
MISSION	*MILITARY ELITE*	*CIVILIAN ELITE*	*MASS PUBLIC*
CONGO	284	484	6,861
IRAQ	6,016	19,045	29,853
TAIWAN	17,425	17,554	20,172

Source: Peter D. Feaver and Christopher Gelpi, "A Look at Casualty Aversion: How Many Deaths Are Acceptable? A Surprising Answer," Washington Post, 7 November 1999.

As the authors point out, one must interpret these averages in general terms and must realize that they do not necessarily reflect the actual casualties the public will accept once real soldiers start dying. But the "sheer numbers" and "dramatic differences" between the groups are significant.[83] More importantly, they are consistent with the previous research that explained public support in terms of ends and means and the democratic conversation. The Taiwan case is a holdover from the cold war and represents deep-rooted American sentiment for the Nationalist Chinese and the "long-standing commitment to defend Taiwan."[84] Many Americans associate defending Taiwan with resisting communism and defending democracy—links that go back to the cold war and World War II, which the public considers very important, if not vital, national interests. It

---

[83] Feaver and Gelpi, B3.
[84] Ibid.

is not surprising, therefore, to find consensus on the costs that all three groups are willing to accept to accomplish the mission.

The Iraq and Congo cases are examples of post-cold-war interventions which have sparked the contention that the American public is casualty-averse. The Iraq case is significant because it demonstrates the effectiveness of leadership and cueing from public leaders. According to the poll, civilian elites claim willingness to accept over three times as many deaths as do military elites. The democratic-conversation model predicts that broad-based support from civilian leaders will influence public opinion. The extremely large number of deaths that the public indicated it would be willing to accept is consistent with the democratic-conversation concept—despite the fact that the reported results from TISS did not imply a direct link between civilian leaders and the public. Feaver and Gelpi postulate that the public's willingness to accept more casualties in Iraq than Taiwan "may reflect lingering traces of successful Bush-Clinton efforts to demonize Saddam Hussein combined with Clinton's attempts to pursue a conciliatory policy toward China."[85] This rationale is also consistent with the premise that cues from public leaders influence and aid the public. The fact that right-center and left-center ideologues from the general public received similar anti-Saddam cues from Bush and Clinton supports the role of leadership in the ends-and-means model.

The Congo scenario arguably encompasses the least vital interests of the three prospective interventions. Likewise, it remains consistent with RAND research predicting that the public will tolerate fewer casualties if the benefits and prospects are not as great. The data shows that the public

---

[85] Ibid.

would tolerate roughly only one-third to one-fourth as many deaths as compared to the Taiwan and Iraq averages. But we must not miss the point that the public was willing to accept over sixty-eight hundred deaths to accomplish the mission. The researchers stated that "the public's estimates for the mission to restore democracy in the Congo were much lower, but were nonetheless substantial. In fact, they were many times higher than the actual casualties suffered by the U.S. military in all post–Cold War military actions combined."[86] The cumulative weight of evidence provided by TISS research is consistent with past public opinion on the role of casualties in prospective or actual conflicts and supports the contention that policy makers and senior military leaders have attributed to the public an aversion to casualties that does not, in fact, exist. The number of deaths that the public indicated it would accept was, in all cases, more than those specified by civilian and military elites. The magnitude of the disparity, as mentioned earlier, has implications for national security and military operations.

Implications for Policy Makers

Our current national security strategy calls for both engagement in the international arena and the use of economic, diplomatic, informational, and military instruments of national power to shape an environment with multiple centers of regional power.[87] In the absence of cold-war-type threats to our national existence, engagement is an attempt by our civilian leadership to prevent the development of pariah states, such as Germany and Japan after World War I, and to reduce the potential for a multifaceted conflict with a nuclear-armed power. These goals

---

[86] Ibid.
[87] A National Security Strategy, 1.

are threatened, however, not by a lack of national resources, but by the casualty-aversion myth working among our policy makers and senior military leaders.

The perception among civilian elites—the policy makers who determine national strategy—that the public is casualty-averse hinders coercive diplomacy and limits military options in support of our national strategy. In fact, James Nathan argues in "The Rise and Decline of Coercive Statecraft" that Clausewitz has been turned "on his head" and that the "current policy theory reverses the Clausewitzian insistence of the supremacy of policy over any autonomous logic attendant to arms."[88] Nathan contends that policy makers have surrendered to the [Caspar] Weinberger Doctrine and [Colin] Powell restrictions on the use of force and that the military has an effective veto over policy options that fall short of vital interests. This flies in the face of a security strategy that champions engagement at a level significantly below vital interests in order to shape the international environment. The effort to shape the environment specifically calls for military actions to prevent challenges to vital interests in the first place.

Nathan contends that the unwillingness of our policy makers to use force to back up diplomacy enfeebles such efforts: "Without a credible capability to use moderate force, fate rather than statecraft determines the future."[89] When tyrants see that our statecraft is weak due to the lack of a "big stick," they remain undeterred. In 1994 a Serbian official commented on the potential introduction of peacekeepers into Bosnia by saying,

---

[88] James Nathan, "The Rise and Decline of Coercive Statecraft," US Naval Institute Proceedings, October 1995, 61–62.
[89] Ibid., 64.

"Clinton has his own problems. . . . He can't afford to have even a few soldiers killed in Bosnia."[90] Statements or actions by our political leaders that demonstrate an unfounded casualty aversion based on the myth of a weak-kneed public weaken coercive diplomacy and embolden future adversaries. As a result, deterrence crumbles, and we must use military forces to contain the Saddam Husseins and Slobodan Milosevics of the world who refuse to heed diplomatic warnings.

A potentially worse scenario than our inability to deter enemies is the potential for policy makers to abandon military force when we need it. As Mark Lorell and Charles Kelley comment, "In the future, a President may elect to delay or forgo direct U.S. military intervention in a Third World conflict—even though it may be needed to defend legitimate U.S. interests—because of concern that public support may decline or collapse once the United States is deeply committed."[91] This fear of casualties among our political leaders encourages renegade world leaders to take risks, based on the potential that their actions will skirt under the threshold of US interests that would elicit a response. If they are successful, engagement is weakened, and other rogue groups will likely test US resolve in areas closer to vital interests. This does not imply that the United States must respond to every disturbance in world harmony but that the decision to respond should be based upon our national security strategy and not upon our need to dispel the myth of casualty aversion.

---

[90] Roger Thurow, "Serbs Bet That West Won't Risk the Thing They Fear: Ground Troops," Wall Street Journal, 21 April 1994, A10. Quoted in Nathan, 63.
[91] Lorell and Kelley, iii.

Implications for Senior Military Leaders

As noted earlier from the TISS study, senior military leaders exhibit an intolerance for casualties that far exceeds the intolerance level of the public and policy makers in typical post-cold-war interventions. Potentially, this has widespread implications for military planning and the military ethos. The Goldwater-Nichols Department of Defense Reorganization Act codified joint war fighting and gave immense responsibility to senior military leaders, especially the war-fighting commanders in chief (CINC). Such responsibility, if tainted by a belief that military action must be casualty free, can have the unintended consequence of shifting the burden of risk to the people our military mission says we should protect.

Of course, legitimate reasons exist for military leaders to tolerate or accept fewer casualties than would the public or political leaders. As Feaver and Gelpi point out, it is entirely rational for "military officers to give lower casualty estimates for nontraditional missions" when "they do not believe those missions are vital to the national interest."[92] Military leaders adhere to the principle of economy of force and do not want to fritter away limited assets on missions that might detract from the ultimate mission of defeating vital threats to national security. The danger, as mentioned earlier, is that military leaders will trump civilian policy and, in a bout of self-interest, "deter" missions that are essential building blocks in the national strategy of engagement.

It is also true that military commanders care about their troops and do not want to waste lives. The conviction that fewer

---

[92] Feaver and Gelpi, B3.

casualties are warranted may indicate that there are better ways to fight than the World War I practice of frontal attacks. Most people agree that we should maximize effective planning and asymmetric strategies, which apply American technological strengths to enemy weaknesses, to dislocate, confuse, and defeat an enemy[93] but that we should not use them as a panacea because of a mistaken belief that the mission must be risk free. As one author stated, "Reduced casualties have always been a goal of a good commander. Yet stating this as an absolute requirement that can be fulfilled by our advanced technology simply ignores the true nature of mankind and war."[94] The argument is not that commanders should avoid unnecessary casualties—duty demands no less. The issue is the impact of excessive casualty aversion on planning and the military ethos.

Deliberate planning at the theater strategic and operational levels of war is the domain of the war-fighting CINCs. If, as this article argues, senior military leaders are casualty-averse or erroneously believe that the American public will not accept losses, this process can be skewed and produce plans that fall short of their intended purpose. The Vietnam legacy for senior officers entails a belief that American lives "were needlessly lost" and a determination "to avoid putting military personnel at risk unless absolutely necessary."[95] The Gulf War corollary

---

[93] For an excellent discussion of asymmetric airpower strategies, see Ronald R. Fogleman, "Advantage USA: Air Power and Asymmetric Force Strategy," Air Power History 42, no. 2 (Summer 1996): 5–13.
[94] Conversino, 21.
[95] Charles J. Dunlap Jr., "Organizational Change and the New Technologies of War" (paper presented at the Joint Services Conference on Professional Ethics, Washington, D.C., January 1998), 9;

states that the American public will not tolerate future operations which promise more than a "handful of casualties."[96] Geographic CINCs and their senior staff officers produce theater engagement plans, write commanders' estimates of the situation, and provide courses of action to the National Command Authorities, all of which are affected by these legacies. Casualty aversion on the part of senior officers, or the erroneous perception that the public demands casualty-free interventions, can produce a self-limiting filter or paradigm through which all plans must pass. One wonders whether Inchon would be possible today—would the plan be found "not acceptable" due to excessive risk?

A potentially greater threat posed by excessive casualty aversion is the destruction of the military ethos. Feaver and Gelpi highlight the views of Donald Snider, a retired Army colonel and West Point professor, who argues that the military ethic "is built on the principles of self-sacrifice and mission accomplishment. Troops are supposed to be willing to die so that civilians do not have to."[97] Charles Dunlap agrees: "Uniformed professionals need to ask themselves whether the military's altruistic ethos, axiomatic to its organizational culture, is being replaced by an occupationalism that places—perhaps unconsciously—undue weight on self-preservation over mission accomplishment."[98] One can best see the degrading impact of casualty aversion in excessive force protection, which shifts mission risk from the US military to others.

---

on-line, Internet, 7 January 2000, available from http://www.usafa.af.mil/jscope/JSCOPE98/Dunlap98.htm.
[96] Conversino, 21.
[97] Feaver and Gelpi, B3.
[98] Dunlap, 10.

The ongoing operations in Kosovo provide an insightful case study on the impact of casualty aversion on mission accomplishment and the military ethic. In a positive example, Lt Col Bruce Gandy, a Marine battalion commander, wrote an article in the Marine Corps Gazette describing his unit's successful operations in Kosovo. His unit filled the vacuum left by retreating Serbian forces and provided security for the local population. He described the mission by saying, "Although we minimized risk wherever we could, we quickly realized force protection cannot be paramount. First and foremost is the mission. Marines must always answer the call to arms no matter what the cost."[99]

The Marine Corps accomplished the mission by decentralizing operations and giving companies control of individual sectors. Companies lived in the areas for which they were responsible, and the company commander acted as the police chief and civil administrator. These decentralized operations quickly gained the trust of the local population, but they were not without risks. Gandy states, "Decentralization while projecting a visible presence is not without risk. Marines are taught to seize the initiative. In peace enforcement operations, this means exposing our Marines and sailors to danger."[100]

In contrast to the mission-focused approach of the Marine Corps, the follow-on Army forces are plagued by excessive force protection and casualty aversion run amuck. In an attempt to drive the casualty rate to zero, the US military is building an isolated, multi-million-dollar compound to provide a

---

[99] Bruce A. Gandy, "Force Protection and Mission Accomplishment," Marine Corps Gazette 83, no. 11 (November 1999): 44.
[100] Ibid., 45.

comfortable, secure environment. Allied soldiers who still live among the people, as marines did previously, ridicule the American compound, calling it "Disneyland."[101] In its mission statement, the brigade responsible for one-fourth of Kosovo lists its foremost objective as "self-protection" while other "peacekeeping tasks, such as maintaining 'a safe and secure environment' and . . . building a civil society receive lesser priority."[102] It is not surprising that the brigade lists self-protection as its first objective, given the fact that the Army's European Command "holds that its primary objective is 'To Protect and Take Care of the Force.' "[103]

The compound in Kosovo is not the issue. The problem is that casualty-averse military leaders have determined that risk avoidance takes precedence over the mission given by American and North Atlantic Treaty Organization (NATO) policy makers and have shifted the risk to our NATO allies and the people of Kosovo. If presence in one sector declines, all of the adjacent areas are in greater danger, and the people in those sectors are at greater risk for reprisals. Even if civilian deaths do not increase, the greatest casualty is the military ethos—the warrior ethic of service before self, willingness to sacrifice for the society we protect, and the responsibility to minimize risk to those whom we protect. Excessive casualty aversion by senior military leaders does not accurately reflect the view of the

---

[101] Jeffrey Smith, "A GI's Home Is His Fortress: High-Security, High-Comfort U.S. Base in Kosovo Stirs Controversy," Washington Post, 5 October 1999, A11.
[102] Ibid.
[103] Jonathan Foreman, "The Casualty Myth," National Review, 3 May 1999, 40.

American public and, instead of protecting the force, may actually be sowing the seeds of its destruction.

Conclusion

The cold war is over, and the world is still a dangerous place. American national security interests are no longer defined by the bipolar confrontation with the Soviet Union, and the threats to our national security are more subtle and hard to describe. As the only remaining superpower, the United States has embarked on the path of engagement— exercising active, decisive leadership in world economics and diplomacy to make the world a more prosperous and democratic entity. By engaging on many levels on which our interests are less than vital, our strategy seeks to preserve our vital interests and status as a superpower.

In a world without a governing authority, however, our ability to engage and resist those who do not share our vision of freedom and prosperity depends on the instrument of military power. At present, the United States has the most powerful armed forces the world has ever seen; but dictators, terrorists, and allies challenge our status as a superpower, based on the perception that a casualty-averse public limits our ability to wield military power.

Research shows that the public is not an irrational mass calling for immediate withdrawal from military interventions at the first news reports showing American deaths. Instead, the public weighs the expected and actual costs with the benefits and prospects for success and makes a decision with the aid of cues from political leaders. Public support is not all-encompassing but can be counted on when civilian leadership adequately frames the debate in terms of a positive ends-and-means calculation. The conventional wisdom that the public is casualty-averse is wrong, but civilian policy makers and military elites still act on the mistaken assumption that the public will no longer accept the risks of military action.

By attributing casualty aversion to the public, civilian and military elites have masked their own aversion to casualties and threaten our status as a superpower. Casualty aversion on the part of civilian leaders renders coercive diplomacy ineffective and undermines deterrence. Casualty aversion on the part of senior military leaders becomes a filter that limits bold options and aggressive plans and insidiously destroys the military ethos. The misinterpretation of public casualty aversion by policy makers and senior military leaders hurts our foreign policy and military credibility. A casualty-aversion myth "is hardly sound footing for American foreign policy"[104] and military operations.

---

[104] Feaver and Gelpi, B3.

The Casualty-Aversion Myth

Lt. Col Richard A. Lacquement, Jr.

The Naval War College Review published this article in its Winter 2004 issue. Lacquement here covers some of the same ground we have already seen in his review of public opinion data, however his piece spends more time with the policy implications of casualty aversion, which he views as being powered by the "myth" of low public tolerance for casualties. The myth "should be vigorously opposed," he argues. Today, Lacquement is a colonel and Director of Military Strategy at the U.S. Army War College.

> It's easy to see. . . . People go off to war and the bands play and the flags fly. And it's not quite so easy when the flag is draped over a coffin coming back through Dover, Delaware. -SENATOR JOHN GLENN, 1997

That is the nature of the American public's sensitivity to U.S. military casualties? How does casualty sensitivity affect the pursuit of American national security objectives?[105] The first question is easy to answer: There is no intrinsic, uncritical casualty aversion among the American public that limits the use of U.S. armed forces. There is a wide range of policy objectives on behalf of which the public is prepared to accept American casualties as a cost of success. Squeamishness about even a few casualties for all but the most important national causes is a

---

[105] Senate Armed Services Committee, Hearing on the Nomination of William Cohen as Secretary of Defense, 22 January 1997, available at pcinegi.udlap.mx/infoUSA/politics/biograph/2142.htm.

myth. Nonetheless, it is a myth that persists as widely accepted conventional wisdom.

The second question is more difficult to answer. Avoidance of casualties is an unassailably desirable objective. It is precisely the natural nobility of the argument that makes it susceptible to misuse in the policy-making process, potentially leading to ineffective or inefficient choices. The persistence of the myth also causes adversaries to misjudge the likely reactions of the United States. In both of these ways, the myth of deep-seated casualty aversion among the American public hinders the pursuit of American national objectives.

The evidence indicates that the public response to casualties is a function of leadership and consensus among national policy elites, who have wide latitude in this area. They should not allow concern about casualties to replace thorough consideration of the larger context of costs and benefits. National leaders must not let unsubstantiated assertions of American casualty aversion distort the national security policy-making process or compromise professional military ethics.

This article briefly describes the nature of American casualty sensitivity, identifies some prominent negative effects of widespread acceptance of the casualty myth, and offers recommendations that may produce a more accurate understanding of the American public's casualty sensitivity.

AMERICAN CASUALTY SENSITIVITY

Are the American people in fact reluctant to risk lives? In a superficial and unhelpful sense, the American public is always reluctant to risk lives, particularly if there is some other reasonable way to accomplish objectives. No one wants casualties.

> We had 500 casualties a week when we [the Nixon administration] came into office. America now is not willing to take any casualties. Vietnam produced a whole new attitude.

> HENRY KISSINGER, 1999

> It's obvious that there's a political agenda to have low casualties. . . . If my Achilles' heel is the low tolerance of the American people for casualties, then I have to recognize that my success or failure in this mission [in Bosnia] is directly affected by that.

> MAJOR GENERAL WILLIAM L. NASH, 1996

> [America is] a nation intolerant of casualties.

> EDWARD LUTTWAK, 1995

> And the hearts that beat so loudly and enthusiastically to do something, to intervene in areas where there is not an immediate threat to our vital interests, when those hearts that had beaten so loudly see the coffins, then they switch, and they say: "What are we doing there?"

SENATOR WILLIAM COHEN (LATER SECRETARY OF DEFENSE)

These are just some of the many similar expressions of the conventional wisdom of American public casualty aversion.[106] The conventional wisdom is strong among civilian, military, and media elites. Steven Kull and I. M. Destler have recorded many interviews-with members of Congress and their staffs, the media, the executive branch, and leaders of nongovernmental organizations-that support this view.[107] Other interviews with members of the media and military leaders also confirm a widespread belief that the American public is unwilling to accept casualties.[108]

---

[106] Henry Kissinger, quoted in C. David Kotok, "Vietnam's Lessons Still Shaping U.S. Policy, Practice," Omaha World-Herald, 14 September 1999, p. 1; Maj. Gen. William Nash quote cited in Rick Atkinson, "Warriors without a War: U.S. Peacekeepers in Bosnia Adjusting to New Tasks: Arbitration, Bluff, Restraint," Washington Post, 14 April 1996, p. A1; Edward N. Luttwak, "Toward Post-Heroic Warfare," Foreign Affairs 74, no. 3 (May/June 1995), p. 115; Senator William Cohen, quoted in Charles Lane, "The Double Man," New Republic, 28 July 1997, available at www.tnr.com/archive/07/072898/lane072897.html (date of original quote not identified).

[107] Steven Kull and I. M. Destler, Misreading the Public: The Myth of a New Isolationism (Washington, D.C.: Brookings Institution Press, 1999). Kull and Destler "conducted a series of eighty three interviews with persons selected from four groups: twelve members and sixteen staff of the U.S. Congress; nineteen officials of the executive branch; eighteen representatives of the media and eighteen senior professionals at nongovernmental organizations" (pp. 25-26).

[108] To clarify the nature of this conventional wisdom among policy elites, I conducted over twenty interviews with members of major news organizations, with particular emphasis on correspondents, producers, and analysts experienced in defense and national security interests. I also conducted interviews with over a dozen senior military leaders (current and former). The focus of the interviews was the

The wellspring of this conventional wisdom is generally understood to be the Vietnam War, as reinforced by experiences in Lebanon (1983) and Somalia (1993). The tremendous efforts by civilian and military leaders to minimize casualties in other operations-the Persian Gulf War (1991), Haiti (1994), Bosnia (1995), and Kosovo (1999)-can be read as a reaction to the public's purported low tolerance for casualties. Rising casualties in Iraq following the end of "major combat operations" have also been portrayed as an important factor affecting the public's willingness to support the mission. The abandonment of military intervention in several instances in which it was seriously considered has also been attributed to casualty aversion. Examples include the Balkans (before 1995), Rwanda (1994), and Zaire/Congo (1995).

Manifestations of this conventional wisdom are many and widespread-the "Vietnam syndrome," the "Dover test," the "CNN effect," part of the Weinberger/Powell doctrine, the concept of "post-heroic warfare," and a social equity effect attributed to the absence of American civilian elites and their children from military service.

The "Vietnam syndrome" is commonly understood as a general reticence among Americans to use military force abroad as a result of negative lessons of the Vietnam experience. It is "that revulsion at the use of military power that afflicted our national psyche for decades after our defeat."[109] It is a comprehensive generalization about the American public's unwillingness to

---

respondents' perceptions of the American public's aversion to casualties.
[109] William Safire, quoted by Richard Falk, "The Vietnam Syndrome," Nation, 9 July 2001.

continue to support U.S. foreign military efforts, particularly as casualties rise. This aspect of the Vietnam syndrome relates casualty aversion to the idea that public support for military operations in Vietnam declined because of the human costs of the war.[110] A variant attributing the decline in popular support to media portrayals of events in Vietnam has fed negative attitudes toward the media, particularly among many members of the military.

Senator John Glenn's "Dover test" (alluded to in the first epigraph, above) refers to the American public's assumed response to American service people returning to the United States in flag-draped coffins. This oft-repeated image symbolizes the cost in casualties of American military operations. In an interesting response to its presumed visceral effect, the Department of Defense has prohibited media coverage of such events since 1989: "There will be no arrival ceremonies for, or media coverage of, deceased military personnel returning to or departing from Dover AFB [Air Force Base] or Ramstein AFB [in Germany], to include interim stops."[111] In a sense, this provides an official endorsement of the presumption that casualties have a powerful effect on the public.

The "CNN effect" refers broadly to the purported impact of certain types of visual images, to include American casualties,

---

[110] Eric V. Larson, "Ends and Means in the Democratic Conversation: Understanding the Role of Casualties in Support for U.S. Military Operations," Ph.D. dissertation, RAND Graduate School, 1996, pp. 33-36.
[111] Defense Press Office, Assistant Secretary of Defense (Public Affairs), "Public Affairs Guidance-Casualty and Mortuary Affairs-Operation Enduring Freedom," 1 November 2001.

when broadcast on the news. Like the Dover test, it suggests that visual images of casualties will elicit an immediate response from the public. Its various formulations convey the idea that the public can respond precipitately to gut-wrenching depictions of human suffering, not only military casualties but starving children and other civilian victims of war.[112] This dynamic is also assumed to induce a similar visceral response to such dramatic pictures as those of the body of an American soldier being dragged through the streets of Mogadishu in 1993.[113]

The Weinberger/Powell doctrine is a set of six tests, drawn in part from the Vietnam War experience, that, its advocates believe, should govern the use of American military power.[114] One test is the presence or absence of the support of the American public and its elected representatives. In policy debates considering the use of force, it is in the framework of

---

[112] For a detailed treatment of this subject, see Susan Moeller, Compassion Fatigue: How the Media Sell Disease, Famine, War and Death (New York: Routledge, 1999).

[113] For one example of this interpretation, Lawrence S. Eagleburger, speaking during a panel discussion on the so-called CNN Effect, "I think there's no question that TV pictures of the dead GI has a lot to do with our leaving." "'The CNN Effect': How 24-Hour News Coverage Affects Government Decisions and Public Opinion," Brookings/Harvard Forum: Press Coverage and the War on Terrorism, transcript of panel discussion, 23 January 2002, available at www.brook.edu/dybdocroot/comm/transcripts/20020123.htm.

[114] Caspar Weinberger, Fighting for Peace: Seven Critical Years in the Pentagon, appendix: "Text of Remarks by Secretary of Defense Weinberger at the National Press Club, November 28, 1984" (New York: Warner Books, 1991), pp. 445-57.

this test that assertions about the willingness of the public to handle casualties enter decision making.[115]

"Post-heroic warfare" is the idea that the scope of casualties resulting from the clash of armies at close quarters is no longer tolerable to the American public. Edward Luttwak asserts that America is "a nation intolerant of casualties";[116] he relates this to the decreasing size of American families in the post-World War II era. Luttwak believes that there exists a powerful unwillingness among Americans to permit military operations that might endanger their children.

Finally, sociologist Charles Moskos posits that the American public's sensitivity is a function of inequitable social relations created by the absence of elite members of society or their children in the ranks of the military. "Only when the privileged classes perform military service does the country define the cause as worth young people's blood. Only when elite youth are on the firing line do war losses become more acceptable."[117]

THE NUANCED REALITY

Nonetheless, there are many interests and national objectives for which Americans have readily found the risk of casualties an acceptable cost. There is in fact no evidence that the public is intrinsically casualty averse. Several studies based on polling

---

[115] For an example of this, see descriptions of General Powell's concerns in Michael R. Gordon and Bernard E. Trainor, The Generals' War: The Inside Story of the Conflict in the Gulf (Boston: Little, Brown, 1995), pp. 34, 130-31.

[116] Luttwak, "Toward Post-Heroic Warfare," p. 115.

[117] Charles Moskos, "Our Will to Fight Depends on Who Is Willing to Die," Wall Street Journal, 20 March 2002, p. A22; Mark Shields, "In Power but Not in Peril," Washington Post, 15 October 2002, p. 19.

data demonstrate that the American public is willing to accept casualties when the need and the likely consequences are explained to them by national leaders. This readiness is not restricted to issues of vital national interests or self-defense. The public takes its lead from how national leaders characterize and justify the mission. Leadership plays a crucial role in influencing how the public responds to casualties.

One of the best studies on this topic is Eric V. Larson's *Casualties and Consensus*.[118] In this detailed study, Larson explores the relationship between public support for military operations and the level of casualties for World War II, Korea, Vietnam, the Dominican Republic, Lebanon, Panama, the 1991-92 Gulf war, and Somalia. The findings are very instructive.

Majorities of the public have historically considered the potential and actual casualties in U.S. wars and military operations to be an important factor in their support, and there is nothing new in this. But the current attention to the public's unwillingness to tolerate casualties misses the larger context in which the issue has become salient: The simplest explanation consistent with the data is that support for U.S. military operations and the willingness to tolerate casualties are based upon a sensible weighing of benefits and costs that is influenced heavily by consensus (or its absence) among political leaders.[119]

---

[118] Eric V. Larson, Casualties and Consensus: The Historical Role of Casualties in Domestic Support for U.S. Military Operations (Santa Monica, Calif.: RAND, 1996). The larger study from which this is drawn is Larson's dissertation, "Ends and Means in the Democratic Conversation: Understanding the Role of Casualties in Support for U.S. Military Operations."
[119] Ibid., p. xv.

Further, casualties do not trigger an immediate public desire for withdrawal from an operation. Both in Vietnam and in Somalia, for example, the public was willing to accept casualties even as the political leaders signaled that the United States would extract itself. The public supported orderly, not precipitous, withdrawal. In both cases, Larson's analysis suggests that an important consideration was the public's support for continued engagement until prisoner or hostage issues were resolved.[120]

In a study that differentiated between the mass public, civilian elites, and military elites, Peter Feaver and Christopher Gelpi found the mass public more willing than policy elites to accept casualties in hypothetical national missions ranging from conventional war to peacekeeping and humanitarian intervention. They also found civilian elites more ready than military leaders to accept casualties in intervention missions short of conventional war.[121]

Polling data indicates that though the American public's willingness to accept casualties is related to the strength of U.S. interests involved, a wide range of justifications is acceptable. The public does not require a direct threat to U.S. or allied security or other such vital interests to endorse the use of armed force. Instead, it supports broader American efforts on behalf of democratization, humanitarian assistance, and cultivation of a favorable international environment for the United States and other nations, including for the United

---

[120] Ibid., p. 66.

[121] Peter Feaver and Christopher Gelpi, "Casualty Aversion: How Many Deaths Are Acceptable? A Surprising Answer," Washington Post, 7 November 1999, p. B3.

Nations and UN peacekeeping.[122] Polling related to operations in Afghanistan as well as with respect to military operations against Iraq also demonstrates robust public support for military operations, even with expectations of casualties.[123] Polling data, then, reinforces what many analyses have noted over the years-Americans are motivated by considerations of both realistic national interests and idealistic international aspirations.[124]

NEGATIVE EFFECTS OF THE CASUALTY-AVERSION ASSERTION

If the response to the supposed casualty aversion is simply the use of alternative means to accomplish the same objective, there is no problem. Unfortunately, perceptions of casualty

---

[122] Kull and Destler, Misreading the Public, pp. 81-112.

[123] For example, see a CBS News Poll released 24 September 2001, based on a nationwide random sample of 1,216 adults, 20-23 September 2001. Before military action began in Afghanistan, 72 percent of the public supported military action against whoever had been responsible for the terrorist attacks, even if that meant "thousands of American military personnel will be killed." ABC News polls since 11 September 2001 also continue to show strong support for military action, even when the public believes there will be significant U.S. military casualties. There is evidence of increasing popular concern about casualties since the end of major combat operations in Iraq. Nonetheless, there is still evidence of strong support for seeing the mission through in the face of mounting casualties. In an August 2003 ABC News poll, 69 percent of those polled favored the statement, "The United States should keep its military forces in Iraq until civil order is restored there, even if that means continued U.S. military casualties," versus 27 percent who favored withdrawal of U.S. military forces even if civil order had not been restored.

[124] For a recent example of this analysis from a somewhat surprising source, see Henry Kissinger, Diplomacy (New York: Simon and Schuster, 1994), pp. 834-35.

aversion can have more negative effects. Misplaced concern on this point can significantly impede the pursuit of national objectives, in four main ways.

Inefficient or Ineffective Execution

Belief that the public cannot withstand casualties can skew choices concerning the use of force in ways that cause operations to be conducted inefficiently or ineffectively. Recent combat operations in Kosovo (1999) and Afghanistan (2001-present) illustrate this point. Another aspect of this negative effect is the manner in which American armed forces, overly concerned about casualties, pursue force protection and "zero defects" to such an extent that mission effectiveness is hindered.

In 1999 in Yugoslavia, NATO found itself in a dilemma partly, if not wholly, based on the priority given to avoiding friendly casualties. On the first night of the war, President William Clinton announced that he did not intend to use ground forces in Kosovo. This knowledge made it possible for the Serbs to hide weapons and troops-forces that otherwise would have been tactically deployed and therefore more easily detectable-from the NATO air campaign. Furthermore, the difficulties in accurately targeting from the mandated fifteen-thousand-foot altitude made accidental civilian deaths and injuries ("collateral damage") more likely. Meanwhile, the Serbian forces (regular, police, and irregular), free to operate near civilian targets that NATO was taking care to avoid, were able to accelerate their efforts to force Kosovar Albanians to leave.

Ultimately, in terms of lost U.S. lives, the Kosovo operation was a resounding success, if not a rapid one. In terms, however, of one of the operation's principal objectives-support for the

Kosovar Albanians and an end to ethnic cleansing and atrocities-the effect was less gratifying. Did an unwillingness to threaten, much less use, ground forces or to deliver lower-level and more accurate aerial attacks exacerbate and extend the suffering of the people we intended to help? A counterfactual but plausible argument suggests that military tactics that would have posed greater risks to friendly forces would also have ended the conflict more swiftly and, quite possibly, with much smaller loss of life overall.

Casualty aversion hindered operational effectiveness in Kosovo in other ways as well. For instance, Task Force HAWK, which combined Apache attack helicopters and the Army Tactical Missile System, was not given permission to attack inside Kosovo because, among other things, Serbian targets, having been dispersed, were no longer appropriate targets for the Apaches, which had been designed to attack massed armored formations. The modest rewards expected from flushing out dispersed Serb units was outweighed in the minds of many Americans involved by the high risk of casualties.[125] An Air Force officer assigned to one of the key NATO intelligence centers said, "If he [Slobodan Milosevic] kills one U.S. pilot, he wins. . . . [H]e knows that, and we know that."[126] This view had much to do with keeping Task Force HAWK sidelined.

---

[125] Dana Priest, "Risks and Restraints: Why the Apaches Never Flew in Kosovo," Washington Post, 29 December 1999, p. A1.

[126] Gen. Dennis Reimer and an unnamed U.S. Air Force officer who provided a classified intelligence briefing on Yugoslav air defense measures for the Apache pilots of Task Force Hawk (assigned to the Joint Analysis Center in Molesworth, United Kingdom), quoted in Sean Naylor, "Sidelined: How America Won a War without the Army," Army Times, 16 August 1999, p. 20.

MASS VERSUS ELITE OPINION

The poll upon which analysts Peter Feaver and Christopher Gelpi based their assertion of the relative willingness of the mass public to countenance casualties was conducted between September 1998 and June 1999. It addressed hypothetical missions to "stabilize a democratic government in Congo," "prevent Iraq from obtaining weapons of mass destruction," and "defend Taiwan against invasion by China." In each case the public identified a higher level of acceptable casualties than did samples of elite military leaders and civilian elite leaders. Significantly, in each case the number of acceptable casualties to the public was in the thousands. The question even included a description of how many casualties the U.S. had actually suffered in Somalia (forty-three), the Gulf War (383), Korea (approximately fifty-four thousand), Vietnam (approximately fifty-eight thousand) and World War II (approximately four hundred thousand). Results:

Highest number of American military deaths acceptable to .		Military Elite	Civilian Elite	Mass Public
	Stabilize democratic government in Congo	284	484	6,861
	Prevent Iraq from obtaining WMD	6,016	19,045	29,853
	Defend Taiwan from Chinese invasion	17,425	17,554	20,172

Polling sample: 623 military officers, 683 nonveteran civilian elites, 1,001 adults from the general public. In addition to Feaver and Gelpi's Washington Post article (note 17), see Triangle Institute for Security Studies, "Project on the Gap between the Military and Civilian Society: Digest of Findings and Studies," Conference on the Military and Civilian Society,

Cantigny Conference Center, 1st Division Museum, 28-29 Oct. 1999, available at

www.poli.duke.edu/civmil/summary_digest.pdf, 8.

The negative effect of excessive casualty aversion was evident in the war in Afghanistan, despite the clear, self-defense justification for the operation and its overwhelming public support.

Addressing the nation when the bombs began to fall on 7 October, Bush said the troops might have to make the ultimate sacrifice of their lives. Despite such warnings, there is some evidence that U.S. officials have questioned whether Americans would accept significant casualties, in spite of polls indicating that they would. An adviser to senior Pentagon officials said concerns about high American casualties led the Bush administration to craft a strategy that relied on air power and small numbers of commandos, as opposed to tens of thousands of American ground troops. "They are risk-averse about casualties," said the adviser, who requested anonymity. "They didn't know what we were facing."[127]

An important cost of this approach was the failure to capture or destroy large numbers of al-Qa'ida and Taliban forces-and possibly Osama Bin Laden himself-during the Tora Bora fight of December 2001.

It was widely acknowledged that the attacks on al-Qa'ida and its Taliban hosts had been forced upon Americans as a matter of self-defense. As after Pearl Harbor, Americans were strongly

---

[127] Tom Bowman, "War Casualties Could Test Public's Resolve," Baltimore Sun, 18 November 2001.

committed to fighting the perpetrators of mass murder and their accomplices. Polls conducted in the months after 11 September 2001 demonstrated willingness to accept the risks of significant ground force operations, even high casualties.[128]

The initial U.S. military forces on the ground included small contingents of special operations forces coordinating the support by American aerial attacks of the operations of Afghan allies. The strategy worked brilliantly in the first phase, unseating the Taliban government and seizing major population centers. However, even when the enemy was pushed into the mountainous hinterlands, the same American strategy continued-a low-level commitment of U.S. ground and air power, in favor of heavy reliance on local coalition partners. In retrospect, it appears that as a result large numbers of enemy soldiers and leaders were able in December 2001 to escape into neighboring Pakistan or remote areas of Afghanistan.[129] Having interests different from those of the American forces, local Afghan coalition members appear to have made deals that permitted these escapes.

[An Afghan] commander, Hajji Zaher, said in an interview in Jalalabad that he had pleaded with Special Forces officers to block the trails to Pakistan. "The Americans would not listen," said Mr. Zaher, 38. "Their attitude was, 'We must kill the enemy, but we must remain absolutely safe.' This is crazy. If they had

---

[128] Gary Langer, "Support for War: Do They Mean It?" Polling Report 17, no. 18 (24 September 2001).
[129] Michael Gordon, "Rumsfeld Burdened by Stilling Echoes of the Grisly Raid in Somalia," New York Times, 7 March 2002.

been willing to take casualties to capture Osama then, perhaps they'd have to take fewer casualties now."[130]

A more substantial American ground force might have crippled al-Qa'ida-that is, would have better achieved the national objective at Tora Bora. A stronger American effort could have rendered ineffective enemy fighters intent on continuing attacks against American or allied forces in Afghanistan, maybe even disrupted or destroyed cells dedicated to further terrorist attacks on the United States itself. The additional risks would have been easy to justify. If casualty aversion among military leaders was a significant factor in this misjudgment, the implication is that the military, for institutionally dysfunctional reasons, may be unwilling to accept prudent risks in the pursuit of national interests-even when public support is unequivocal.

This unhealthy state of affairs is a factor not only at the upper levels of military and civilian leadership. As emphasis on risk avoidance filters down the chain of command, junior commanders and their soldiers become aware that low-risk behavior is expected and act accordingly. As Brigadier General Daniel Kaufman, dean of academics at the U.S. Military Academy at West Point, has said,

What it [priority on force protection] says is officers no longer have the right to use their judgment, to make decisions based on the situation on the ground and act decisively in accordance with what they believe to be the requirements of carrying out their mission. You do not deploy somewhere to protect yourself. If you want to do that you stay in Kansas. You deploy

---

[130] John F. Burns, "10-Month bin Laden Mystery: Dead or Alive?" New York Times, 30 September 2002, p. A1.

somewhere to accomplish a mission. And, oh, by the way, an ancillary part of that is you never put your soldiers in harm's way recklessly, but you understand that in operations that's the nature of war.[131]

Concerned about the effects of any casualties, then, commanders and small-unit leaders become hesitant to act, fearing that even small events at the tactical level could have important strategic effects.[132]

Recent studies have revealed the existence in the services of a degree of safety consciousness and focus on risk assessment that reinforces risk aversion in general.[133] To prevent the automatic investigations and presumptions of error that attend any death-in peace or war-commanders make tremendous efforts to avoid such an event and, in some cases, to shield themselves from blame if a fatality does occur. Such efforts, however well intentioned or understandable in themselves, are inappropriate and even professionally unethical if they override mission accomplishment. "Force protectionism" as an end in

---

[131] Serge Schmemann, "Word for Word/The Long Gray Line: For Tomorrow's Army, Cadets Full of Questions," New York Times, 8 July 2001, "Week in Review," p. 1.

[132] Atkinson, "Warriors without a War," p. A1. The article describes the concerns of commanders that any casualties will have a tremendous impact on the mission, even the cancellation of the mission and the withdrawal of U.S. forces. Consequently, there is tremendous anxiety about force protection and the actions of even the most junior members of the peacekeeping force. The point is reinforced by the high-level attention paid to the first fatality of the operation, a sergeant killed trying to disarm a land mine against orders.

[133] Center for Strategic and International Studies, American Military Culture in the Twenty-first Century, Report of the CSIS International Security Program (Washington, D.C.: CSIS, February 2000).

itself can corrupt professional standards of service to society, as represented by the assignment of the mission in the first place.[134] It places the interests of the members of the armed forces and of the institutions themselves first, and the mission second.

Emboldening Adversaries

Another negative effect of embracing the unsupported conventional wisdom on casualty aversion is that it needlessly encourages American adversaries. With respect to the 1999 war in Kosovo, the NATO commander, General Wesley Clark, observed,

There was continuous commentary on the fear of NATO to accept military casualties. This, unfortunately, is unlikely to be unique to this operation. Of course, using friendly personnel on the ground risks friendly casualties. Neither political nor military leaders will want to take these risks. But our adversaries will exploit our reluctance by facing us with the dilemma of either inflicting accidental injuries to civilians or risking our own people on their territory.[135]

There are numerous examples of the perception by foreigners that the United States is unwilling to risk casualties.[136] This

---

[134] Don M. Snider, John A. Nagl, and Tony Pfaff, Army Professionalism, the Military Ethic and Officership in the 21st Century (Carlisle, Penna.: Strategic Studies Institute, U.S. Army War College, 1999).

[135] Wesley K. Clark, Waging Modern War: Bosnia, Kosovo, and the Future of Combat (New York: PublicAffairs, 2001), p. 436.

[136] Many instances of the conventional wisdom on U.S. casualty aversion have been voiced by foreigners. Examples include: an Indian commentator on the Gulf War cited in Thomas G. Mahnken, "America's Next War," Washington Quarterly 16, no. 3 (Summer

perception has been a factor in the considerations of the nation's enemies. Saddam Hussein before the 1991 Gulf War, Slobodan Milosevic before the Kosovo War in 1999, and Osama Bin Laden and al-Qa'ida generally in 2001 all appear to have had great confidence that the United States lacked the moral courage to face a deadly military confrontation. This assurance made them less susceptible to diplomatic maneuvers or military threats. They seem to have considered the prospect of U.S. military action, particularly the use of ground troops, a bluff.

During the first Gulf war, it appears that the central element of Saddam's strategy was to keep his forces in place during the air war and wait for the ground attack, when, he believed, they would be able to inflict massive casualties and therefore cause the United States to give up. "Saddam Hussein clearly believed that his greatest chance of success lay in inflicting the maximum number of casualties on coalition forces through close combat."[137] In the 2003 war, the apparent Iraqi plan to draw the coalition into an urban battle in Baghdad seemed to have presumed that the Iraqi army would cause unacceptable U.S. casualties. The guerrilla-style war that (at this writing) still continues in Iraq, whether representing the organized resistance of remnants of the former regime or external terrorist groups, also seems based on the premise that simply

---

1993), p. 171; the commander of Iran's Revolutionary Guard Corps and a senior Chinese government official cited in John A. Gentry, "Military Force in an Age of National Cowardice," Washington Quarterly 21, no. 4 (Autumn 1998), p. 179; a European diplomat cited by Justin Brown, "Risks of Waging Only Risk-Free War," Christian Science Monitor, 24 May 2000, p. 1; and the prominent British military historian John Keegan, cited in Atkinson, "Warriors without War," p. A1.
[137] Mahnken, "America's Next War," p. 171.

inflicting casualties on American forces will break the will of the American public and thereby lead to withdrawal.

The supposed American glass jaw with respect to casualties is often connected to the battle in Mogadishu, the capital of Somalia, in 1993. In another incident that seemed to reinforce this point, Haitian thugs prevented the USS Harlan County (LST 1196) docking and offloading troops in Port-au-Prince just a week after the battle in Mogadishu.[138] Osama Bin Laden was to cite Somalia as a reason to expect to be able to force the United States to withdraw from the Middle East. In his 1996 declaration of war on the United States, Osama Bin Laden dismissed the idea that the United States would be able to sustain support for a military response if it suffered casualties.

Your most disgraceful case was in Somalia, where after vigorous propaganda about the power of the USA and its post cold war leadership of the new world order you moved tens of thousands of international force, including twenty eight thousand American soldiers into Somalia. However, when tens of your soldiers were killed in minor battles and one American Pilot was dragged in the streets of Mogadishu you left the area carrying disappointment, humiliation, defeat and your dead with you. Clinton appeared in front of the whole world threatening and promising revenge, but these threats were merely a preparation for withdrawal. You have been disgraced by Allah and you

---

[138] David Halberstam, War in a Time of Peace (New York: Scribner's, 2001), pp. 271-73.

withdrew; the extent of your impotence and weaknesses became very clear.[139]

To Bin Laden, the fact that the bombings in 1998 of two U.S. embassies in Africa elicited only cruise missile attacks in retaliation was further confirmation of this weakness.[140] Ultimately, the planners of the suicide attacks launched against the USS Cole and then the World Trade Center and Pentagon appear to have relied heavily on the presumption of acute casualty sensitivity by Americans.[141] In an October 2001 al-Qa'ida videotape (released just as the U.S. attacks on Afghanistan commenced), Osama Bin Laden's lieutenant, Ayman Zawahri, expressed a conviction that the American will to fight would weaken quickly after a few casualties. The United States would retreat, just as it had "fled in panic from Lebanon and Somalia."[142]

Casualty/Technology Trade-offs, Force Structure, and Weapon Programs

The American way of war has long been characterized by a search for ways to substitute firepower for manpower.[143] In its

---

[139] Osama Bin Laden, "Declaration of War against the Americans Occupying the Land of the Two Holy Places," 23 August 1996, available at www.comw.org/pda/fulltext/960823binladen.html.

[140] Avigdor Haselkorn, "Martyrdom: The Most Powerful Weapon," Los Angeles Times, 3 December 2000, p. M5.

[141] Ibid.

[142] Ayman Zawahri, quoted in James S. Robbins, "Chinook Down," National Review Online, 5 March 2002, available at www.nationalreview .com/robbins/robbins030502.asp.

[143] Russell Weigley, The American Way of War: A History of the United States Military Strategy and Policy (Bloomington: Indiana Univ. Press, 1973), p. xii.

most recent manifestation, this laudable quest has emphasized the utility of airpower, applied at stand-off range, to accomplish coercive aims. Airpower has been a valuable force multiplier for the United States and is regularly advocated in terms not only of effectiveness but of the higher casualties that ground operations would likely produce. Stating the argument directly, Edward Luttwak has suggested that the United States focus more on the development of long-range attack forces, particularly aviation, as an alternative to ground forces, which he asserts are less usable in practice because of casualty aversion on the part of the American public.[144]

Casualty-aversion arguments also provide convenient support for a variety of particular weapons programs. A typical example is the Crusader artillery program. Informed that the system was under consideration for cancellation, Army officials attempted to defend the system by lobbying members of Congress that its termination would put soldiers' lives "at risk."[145] This argument, however, was more sensitive than the Army knew and seems to have had much to do with the rather nasty and public manner in which the issue was finally resolved: the cancellation occurred more swiftly than originally envisioned, the Army was flailed in public, and the person responsible for drafting the "talking points" lost his job.[146]

Another example was opposition to STREETFIGHTER, a prospective naval weapon system, on the premise that it posed

---

[144] Luttwak, "A Post-Heroic Military Policy," pp. 33-44.
[145] Rowan Scarborough, "Army Investigating Officials Who Defended Crusader," Washington Times, 4 May 2002, available at www .washtimes.com/national/20020504 -13602565.htm.
[146] Ibid. and Joe Burlas, "Civilian Deputy Resigns over Crusader Flap," Army News Service, 10 May 2002.

a casualty risk. The concept was to complement the small number of high-cost large warships that currently dominate the Navy force structure with more numerous, smaller ships. Like the PT boats of World War II, these boats would provide flexibility and a capability to attack close to shore. Larger numbers and smaller crews make individual STREETFIGHTER ships less indispensable to the overall force. Unlike the PT boats of World War II, however, they would not be expendable-because of the potential effect of the loss of even their small crews.[147]

Exaggerated concern about casualties can inhibit the selection and development of new systems that can add important capabilities and improve the effectiveness of the armed forces. It may also impede the progress of transformational tactics and approaches-swarming, dispersed operations, network-centric warfare-that by their nature would not provide the degree of force protection afforded by large platforms and massed formations.

Self-Constraint in the Use of Armed Forces

Another negative effect is the failure or reluctance to use the U.S. armed forces at all, due to mistaken beliefs about the public's likely response. To the degree that policy makers believe that the American public cannot endure casualties, leaders may well decide that the risk of casualties is disproportionate to the value of an objective and refrain from taking action in situations. This effect was apparent in debate

---

[147] Greg Jaffe, "Risk Assessment: Plans for a Small Ship Pose Big Questions for the U.S. Navy-The Street Fighter Would Add Punch in Close Combat; Are Deaths Acceptable?" Wall Street Journal, 11 July 2001, p. A1.

over use of force in Bosnia (1992-94) and in Rwanda (1994).[148] Failure to intervene probably saved U.S. lives, but counterfactual (yet plausible) scenarios in both cases suggest that hundreds of thousands of lives could have been saved by intervention, and peace and stability reestablished much earlier.

Assertions of casualty aversion may simply reflect the normative preference of individuals for what the public ought to find acceptable or not. Speaking of the pursuit of Serb war criminals under the Dayton accords, the former commander of the Implementation Force in Bosnia, Admiral Leighton Smith, gives an example:

What's it going to take and what's it going to cost? Then I've got to feed that back to the politicians. . . . "All right, you want me to do this, this is the price." Remember what I said about the war criminals [whom the military might be asked to arrest]? "You want me to do that, it's going to cost you lives. We're going to get people killed doing this. I might have to go to Kansas and tell Johnny's mama that he got his head blown off trying to arrest [Ratko] Mladic [a Bosnian Serb military leader and indicted war criminal] in a coffee shop somewhere. Or better, in a bunker."[149]

In this formulation, it is not a matter of whether the public is willing to accept casualties but this officer's opinion that the

---

[148] For Bosnia, Luttwak, "A Post-Heroic Military Policy," p. 39. For Rwanda, Steven Livingston, in comments during panel discussion, "The CNN Effect," BrookingsHarvard Forum, 23 January 2002.
[149] Leighton W. Smith, Jr. [Adm., USN], interview by Harry Kreisler, "Shaping the U.S. Role in Peacekeeping Operations," University of California Conversations with History, 1 April 1997, available at globetrotter.berkeley .edu/conversations/LWSmith/.

public ought not to accept casualties for this mission. In this way the public's supposed casualty aversion may become a screen for other objections to a particular mission. It may be easier and more morally persuasive to invoke casualty concerns than to pursue a complex or sensitive argument.

POLICY APPLICATIONS

The concept of the American public's casualty aversion is a myth-an inappropriate oversimplification of an important issue. The fundamental policy need is to reject this oversimplification-leaders must understand the more complex reality of the public's reaction to casualties, a reality that in fact affords wide latitude. With a better grasp of this issue, national leaders can avoid errors that distort the policy-making process and corrupt professional military ethics.

Latitude for Leadership

The likely response of the American public to casualties is primarily an issue of leadership. As many studies have noted, even when support for a military operation wanes over time there is no compelling evidence that the public expects either immediate withdrawal or escalation simply in response to casualties. The American public weighs the costs and benefits of the use of force, and the interests involved. In general the public takes a permissive view, one that allows national leaders tremendous discretion to launch military operations and to persevere in them even as casualties mount. It's about leadership.

Elected civilian leaders play a critical role in shaping the public's response to casualties and in characterizing the missions for which they may be incurred. The dynamic is somewhat circular-

the extent of public willingness to abide casualties is a function of the degree of consensus among policy leaders, whereas public reaction to cost has much to do with how elites present the situation. Congressional leaders and their agreement with the administration, or lack of it, have an important effect on the public's sensitivity to casualties. Average citizens perceive policy elites-privy to classified material and detailed analysis, subjected to innumerable inputs from interest and advocacy groups, and served by extensive staffs-as better placed than themselves to weigh costs and benefits. Unsurprisingly, opinion on such major issues as the use of force reflects a "follower effect," whereby individuals take their cues from the nation's civilian and military leaders. There is also evidence that members of political parties tend to favor the positions and policies supported by their parties' leaders-particularly when those leaders include the president.[150]

This understanding also reveals a certain circularity in the Weinberger/Powell rules-that is, though it is undeniably desirable to have American public support for any military operation, the public takes its cue from the political leadership as a whole. Broad agreement among national leaders tends to give the public confidence that the costs of action, including casualties, are being incurred in support of important national interests. If the country's leaders are unsure, the public is unlikely to accept the price willingly.

The public's tolerance for a particular level of casualties in a specific case is not predictable. Moreover, there is considerable

---

[150] For descriptions and discussion of the follower effect, see John E. Mueller, War, Presidents and Public Opinion (New York: Wiley, 1973), pp. 69-74, 122-40; and Larson, Casualties and Consensus, pp. 76-79.

evidence that casualties exceeding original expectations may generate greater scrutiny over military operations in question, without changing the commitment to the objectives sought. In fact, it is common for such sacrifices to cement more firmly the commitment of those who favored force in the first place. Casualties already suffered, far from being dismissed as "sunk costs," are often perceived as requiring redemption, increasing the value of the original purpose.

Not only are the dynamics of casualties difficult to anticipate, there is a natural tendency in the midst of war for casualties to trigger passions that can overwhelm reasoned consideration of government policy. It is valuable to recall Clausewitz's metaphor of the "remarkable trinity" of passion, creativity, and reason:

As a total phenomenon its dominant tendencies always make war a remarkable trinity-composed of primordial violence, hatred, and enmity, which are to be regarded as a blind natural force; of the play of chance and probability within which the creative spirit is free to roam; and of its element of subordination, as an instrument of policy, which makes it subject to reason alone.[151]

Policy makers are responsible for managing the application of reason in the realm of war. This responsibility extends to a clear-headed understanding of the costs and benefits of military operations and the manner in which their results are likely to shape the public attitude.

---

[151] Carl von Clausewitz, On War, ed. Michael E. Howard and Peter Paret (Princeton, N.J.: Princeton Univ. Press, 1976), p. 87.

The Cost-Benefit Policy Equation

A nuanced understanding of the public's willingness to accept casualties should frame the policy process. Leaders should be careful not to let overemphasis on casualty avoidance lead to risk-averse behavior that jeopardizes American policy interests. A misperception of the public's willingness to accept casualties distorts the cost-benefit calculations of civilian and military leaders as they consider when to use military force and how. As General Edward Meyer, former Chief of Staff of the Army, has warned, "No commander likes to lose soldiers, but if he starts out with [no casualties] as his goal, nobody is going to accomplish anything."[152]

The public's understanding of casualties is neither capricious nor fickle. The emotional commitment of liberal societies to the dignity and worth of individuals is part of the foundation of those societies. Human costs weigh heavily-but not too heavily. The public understands and accepts that risks to individuals are sometimes required by the larger interests of society. The public wants to minimize casualties-not just among members of the American military but also innocent civilians and sometimes even enemy combatants. However, as numerous studies have shown, the public understands in essence Clausewitz's dictum that "war is merely the continuation of policy by other means."[153] Military force is used as a means to a policy end; it is difficult to consider the costs (of which casualties are but one) in isolation from the benefits sought. This is true both in the midst of conflicts (for example, Korea and Vietnam) and in the

---

[152] Quoted in Dan Fesperman, "'Casualty Aversion' Overcome by Terror," Baltimore Sun, 17 September 2001, p. 1A.
[153] Clausewitz, On War, p. 89.

consideration of future military operations. It is extremely difficult to articulate succinctly and in advance all possible ends of policy against which casualties might be measured. Moreover, the value of each new casualty is of uncertain subjective weight that varies tremendously from one citizen to the next.

Evocations of the casualty-aversion assertion by national leaders can, as we have seen, cause serious problems. They can embolden adversaries and cause them to overestimate the strategic value of inflicting casualties. They can undermine the deterrent effect of American threats that otherwise might have averted the use of force. Casualty aversion can also give the impression that the United States is trying to shift to allies casualty risks that it is unwilling to accept itself.

Technology has significant drawbacks here; the technology/casualty trade-off debate has been a long one. Again, it is perfectly laudable to pursue methods that minimize casualties; arguing the converse would be ludicrous. More important, however, are the strategic effectiveness and opportunity costs that accrue from the use of various military instruments in singular, sequential or synchronized ways. The casualty-aversion issue can become a surrogate for decades-old interservice arguments between airpower and ground-power advocates. Such often-misdirected disputes focus on the special interests and constituencies of particular means at the expense of national strategic ends. That an option is ostensibly cheaper should not relieve it from the ultimate tests of military effectiveness in achieving national ends. The conviction that technology can or must substitute for risk to human life has a pernicious tendency to distort the consideration of risks and rewards. Cheaper, less risky means may also make more likely the use of force in situations of marginal importance-in which the prestige and effectiveness of the United States and its allies may require escalation to achieve success.[154]

The Professional Military Ethic

How the American public is likely to react to casualties in a particular case is not within the scope of military judgment; officers must stick to their own professional expertise and ethics when rendering advice on the use of armed forces. One reason that concern about casualties has been allowed to cross over into military planning is the Weinberger/Powell doctrine. In particular, its fifth test-which requires "reasonable assurance we will have the support of the American people"-seems to require judgment by national security planners about American public opinion.[155]

Predicting the likelihood and magnitude of casualties in a particular mission is in itself an appropriate professional judgment, firmly grounded in expert knowledge and military experience. Assessments of the impact of casualties on military effectiveness are similarly appropriate; for example, a planner would properly recommend against a course of action in which casualties were likely to render the force unable to complete the mission. However, judgments of the "social weight" of

---

[154] A good example of this is the dynamic of the Kosovo intervention. The initial hope was to use only limited airpower, but lack of quick success increased the willingness to escalate, even to include ground forces, which had been ruled out at the beginning. See Halberstam, War in a Time of Peace, pp. 468-78.

[155] Quoted in Suzanne C. Nielsen, "Rules of the Game? The Weinberger Doctrine and the American Use of Force," in The Future of the Army Profession, Don M. Snider and Gayle L. Watkins, project directors (Boston: McGraw-Hill, 2002), p. 216.

casualties or their effect on public opinion are matters for civilian leaders.

Of course, urging civilian leaders to consider that factor in their decisions to use armed force is appropriate. It is a very weighty matter, touching on important values; military leaders should be confident that civilian leaders have carefully addressed it. However, suggesting in advance what level of casualties, if any, the American public would accept, as an element of considered military judgment, is inappropriate. It represents a corruption of the professional military ethic. Military leaders should recognize the issue of casualty sensitivity for what it is-a question of how potential costs will be valued in terms of policy aims. "If a military officer expresses preferences among policy goals while acting in an official capacity, that officer may come to be seen as more a political figure than a military expert."[156] Such a reputation would undermine the professional credibility of the officer on other issues.[157] There is no objective, a priori standard for predicting the American public's toleration of casualties on behalf of national interests-vital, important, routine, or otherwise.

There is no doubt that military leaders have a profound responsibility to their subordinates and to society more broadly to minimize casualties and take all prudent and reasonable measures to protect the precious human resources entrusted to their care. As servants of society, senior officers are obliged to provide the best possible professional assessment of military

---

[156] Ibid., p. 218.
[157] Ibid., p. 219.

alternatives and their likely costs. Advice on military capacity to achieve objectives is appropriate; opinions as to whether the costs or risks are acceptable exceed the professional responsibility of officers.

This is a significant civil-military relations issue. Assessment of the military costs and risks of a given operation in support of national policy is an appropriate element of professional military judgment and the management of violence, what Clausewitz called the "grammar of war."[158] To decide whether the costs and risks are worth it is to judge the policy itself. That is a decision reserved for civilian leaders.

CONCLUSION

Public casualty aversion is a myth. There is no evidence that the American public has an intrinsic, uncritical aversion to U.S. military casualties. There is strong evidence that the American public seriously considers the costs and benefits of particular missions and that it judges the acceptability of casualties against the value of objectives. Historically, the relationship between public support for military operations vis-a-vis the level of casualties has been a function of national leadership.

The myth's persistence as widespread conventional wisdom is harmful and should be vigorously opposed. The myth impedes efforts to achieve national objectives. National leaders-civilian and military-should work to dispel the presumption that the American public will not endure military casualties; this would place debates on national objectives on a firmer foundation. Dispelling the casualty-aversion myth would allow more precise

---

[158] Clausewitz, On War, p. 605.

and appropriate consideration of when to use military force, more effective and efficient political and military decisions, and more accurately communicate American resolve to potential adversaries.